WHY CHRISTIANS CAN WEAR PANTS

*Spiritual Lessons
from Strange Stories
in Papal History*

Rev. Conrad T. Murphy

En Route Books and Media, LLC
St. Louis, MO

⊕*ENROUTE*
Make the time

En Route Books and Media, LLC

5705 Rhodes Avenue

St. Louis, MO 63109

Contact us at

contactus@enroutebooksandmedia.com

Front Cover: Detail of a 19th-century Bulgarian Icon of Saints Cyril and Methodius by Atanas Karkliyski showing the evangelization of Boris I of Bulgaria (wearing pants). Back Cover: Detail from the 15th-century fresco of Peter receiving the keys by Pietro Perugino.

Copyright 2024 Conrad T. Murphy

ISBN-13: 979-8-88870-246-8

Library of Congress Control Number: 2024947923

Acknowledgments

As with any project, large or small, there are many people who need to be thanked for bringing this book to completion. In a general way, I need to acknowledge my friends and family who encouraged me in this project, from its first inception as a podcast series to the book before you. My immediate family of course has been tremendously supportive, as have priest and lay friends and the Religious Sisters of Mercy of Alma, MI.

Those who more directly contributed to this book though deserve special recognition. Thank you to the team at Catholic CAST Media who supported the initial Habemus Papam Podcast, especially Fr. George Elliot and Leslie Rodriguez. Thank you to Fr. Christopher Seith, Fr. Carter Griffin, and Fr. Paul Scalia for advice and help with navigating the Catholic publishing world. Thank you to Dr. Sebastian Mahfood and Enroute Publishing. Thank you to everyone who helped read initial drafts and gave feedback and edits, especially David Dry, Grace Hegarty, Sr. Marirose Rudek, RSM, Christine Johnson, and Paige Hochschild.

Finally, this book was inspired by and dedicated to the Catholic Terps of the University of Maryland Catholic Student Center.

Table of Contents

Introduction

How many Popes were named John? It seems like a simple question. Putting aside the two John Pauls, our most recent Pope John was Saint John XXIII who died in 1963. So, it would stand to reason that there would be twenty-three popes named John.

Except there aren't. There were only twenty-one. How does that work out?

We can get down to twenty-two fairly easily. Pope John XVI is now recognized as an anti-pope, meaning that at one time he may have been considered by some historians as pope, but we now know that his election was illegitimate. The man who called himself John XVI took power in the middle of a struggle between the Holy Roman Emperor Otto III and local Roman nobles over who really controlled the papacy. John XVI had ousted the legitimate Pope, Greogory V and though he pretended to be the Bishop of Rome for almost a year, we now understand that his papacy was never legitimate. So, that accounts for one of the gaps in the numbering.

Getting down to twenty-one is even stranger and more academic than a medieval power struggle and illegitimate popes. There is neither a pope nor an antipope named John XX. The bishop who became John XXI deliberately skipped XX entirely and went straight to XXI. What's going on?

In September of 1276, Cardinal Pedro Julião of Portugal faced an interesting decision. He had just been elected pope by the cardinals in a conclave which took place in the Italian town of Viterbo, just outside of Rome. Cardinal Julião wanted to take the name John as his papal name. The last pope named John was Pope John XIX who served as Pope in the middle of the 11th century, so it stood to reason that Cardinal Julião would take the name John XX. But the Cardinal had a dangerous piece of knowledge that swayed his decision. At some point in his formation, he had read the catalogue of papal history, the *Liber Pontificalis*, and in that list of the popes he noticed a discrepancy: there were two Pope John XIVs. Someone had made a mistake, and all the popes named John afterwards must be off by one number. So, Cardinal Julião decided to correct the historical record, and took the name John XXI. It seemed like a simple solution to a fairly trivial, yet admittedly nagging, historical inaccuracy. The only problem was that Cardinal Julião was wrong.

The *Liber Pontificalis* listed two Pope John XIVs because the author accounted for John XIV's time as freely exercising his papacy and his time in prison at the mercy of the antipope Boniface VII. But Cardinal Julião didn't realize this; he (and it seems like some of the clergy around him) thought there were two different popes and thus an error in the numbering. So, wanting to correct a historical inaccuracy and get the numbers right, he erroneously skipped XX and went straight to XXI. Thus, we have no John XX and only twenty-one popes named John, not twenty-three.[1] A little knowledge truly is a dangerous thing!

---

[1] Ironically, when John XXIII chose his name, he also did so in part to correct the historical record, to confirm once and for all that another man who claimed to be Pope John XXIII in the 15th century was an antipope. He explained his choice saying, "Twenty-two Johns of indisputable legitimacy have [been Pope], and almost all had a brief pontificate. We

I chose this rather trivial story of papal history to start this book, not only because it is so delightfully arcane and ridiculous, but because it can tell us a lot about the papacy. Pulling the threads of the strange numerology of popes named John we encounter the importance of the papacy and the political struggles to control it, the martyrdoms of some of the occupants of the Chair of Peter and their struggles against the pressures of the world, and the imperfection and humanity of those who hold this august and inspiring office. All while being able to tell a delightful and trivial story.

It's a truth of human nature that we best learn through stories. Our Lord knew this and was constantly using tales and images that were accessible to the people of his time to in some way convey the incredible mysteries of divine love. You've probably been told that God loves you and forgives you, but hearing that God loves you as tenderly and powerfully as a good father who only wants his lost son home, roots the concept deeply in the soul. Several years ago, I was struggling with a concept in spiritual direction, and my director compared the situation to a scene in *The Lord of the Rings*, my favorite book. Immediately it clicked; he was speaking a language I could understand!

Over the past several years, I have been reading and studying the history of the papacy, and amidst the whirling of political in-

---

have preferred to hide the smallness of our name behind this magnificent succession of Roman Popes." "Religion: I Choose John...", Time, November 10, 1958, accessed September 25, 2024, https://time.com/archive/6871154/religion-i-choose-john/. Which, of course, as we now know is itself historically inaccurate. There were only twenty Johns of indisputable legitimacy!

trigues and the drama of degradation and reform, what I discovered was an abundance of fantastic stories. There were popes who were edifying, popes in ridiculous situations, popes who accomplished incredible feats, and even popes who wrote about the morality of wearing pants. So many of these stories I had never heard, and they were so interesting and gave such great insight into the faith. They also humanized these great shepherds of the church, often opening a window to the man himself, acting as best he could in difficult or humbling situations. They brought home the incarnate nature of the Church, put flesh on the characters who have been used by the Holy Spirit to perpetuate and spread the Gospel of Christ.

This book is a collection of some of the best of these Papal stories. In each case, I have done the best I can to use the most accurate historical data available. There are times, however, when an overly scrupulous historical sense gets in the way of a good story. In such situations, I err on the side of the story, because the goal of this book is not primarily historical but theological. I hope to use the adventures of the pope selected to unlock a little more clearly some aspect of our faith than a straight reading of the Catechism might. The reflections will be by their nature eclectic rather than systematic, as they are drawn from the stories and not the other way around. They will be as well the fruits of my own personal meditation and reflection, but in each case, they will touch on some aspects of the great truths of our faith.

In his biography of Saint Francis, the great Catholic author G.K. Chesterton noted that because St. Francis is closer to us both historically and humanly than Jesus, the stories of his life provide an easier entry point into the mysteries of Christ than perhaps even a reading of scripture might. In our weakness as humans, we need to hear things in our own language, with our own human idioms in order to come to comprehension and belief in the difficult truths which are beyond our human capacity. For this reason, Christ became a man, to speak to us as one of us. And for this same reason Christ is continually building up his body the Church, so that each member can be an entry point into that fundamental relationship with Christ, which is the source of our joy. I hope and pray that these strange little stories, as esoteric and at times truly bizarre they may be, facilitate that deeper communication with Christ. Chesterton asserted that St. Francis takes nothing away from Christ, he instead leads people closer. He writes, "If men find certain riddles and hard sayings in the story of Galilee, and if they find the answers to those riddles in the story of Assisi, it really does show that a secret has been handed down in one religious tradition and no other. It shows that the casket that was locked in Palestine can be unlocked in Umbria; for the Church is the keeper of the keys."[2]

---

[2] G.K. Chesterton, *Saint Francis of Assisi*, 135.

Chapter 1

St. Nicholas I and the Question of Trousers

An Ancient Q&A

When one looks through the letters of the great Pope Saint Nicholas I, one comes across the following rather strange sentence,

We consider what you asked about pants to be irrelevant; for we do not wish the exterior style of your clothing to be changed, but rather the behavior of the inner man within you, nor do we desire to know what you are wearing except Christ — for however many of you have been baptized in Christ, have put on Christ [Gal. 3:27] — but rather how you are progressing in faith and good works.[1]

The great pope spends the next paragraph or so of his letter discoursing on the theological significance (or lack thereof) of wearing pants. He continues, acknowledging that though there is not a particular reason why one ought to wear or not wear pants, there is some spiritual significance to this choice of garment. "It should be noted that we put on pants spiritually, when we restrain the lust of the flesh through abstinence; for those places are con-

---

[1] Pope Nicholas I, "The Responses of Pope Nicholas I to the Questions of the Bulgars A.D. 866 (Letter 99)", *Fordham Medieval Sourcebook*, https://sourcebooks.fordham.edu/basis/866nicholas-bulgar.asp

strained by pants in which the seats of luxury are known to be."[2] What prompted such a strange paragraph of papal teaching and what can it tell us about our faith today?

Nicholas I was consecrated the Bishop of Rome on April 24, 858 AD, during a time of profound tension between the west and the east. A dispute had arisen in the Byzantine Empire over the legitimacy of the Patriarch of Constantinople, a man named Photius. The previous patriarch, a strict and conservative bishop named Ignatius, had been deposed by the emperor Michael at the prompting of his uncle. Michael then promoted Photius, a layman and state official, to the position. Ignatius, with the backing of his own faction and the support of the emperor's mother, protested to Rome that he was unfairly deposed, and that Photius's election was likewise illegitimate. After some back and forth, Pope Nicholas sided with Ignatius, and ordered that Photius be deposed. Now, of course, Photius and the Emperor Michael weren't going to be bossed around by some bishop in Rome, even if he is the pope. So, what began as a tense situation, became an all-out schism, with Photius refusing to acknowledge Pope Nicholas, and the Pope demanding the resignation of Photius.

Into this messy conflict walked the Bulgars. The Bulgars were a Slavic tribe which had moved from central Asia into the Balkans (the area which is now today named after them, Bulgaria). This brought them swiftly into conflict with the Byzantine Empire. The Bulgars were originally pagans, but by the ninth century, their ruler, Kahn Boris, began to think about converting to Christianity.

_____

[2] Nicholas I, "Response."

Partly this was because of the growing influence of Christians in Bulgar territory, and partly because it would help Boris politically.[3] With the Church split in a schism between Photius and Nicholas, the burning question at the time was, which side would they take? Which direction would Boris look for guidance in his faith, west to Rome or east to Constantinople?

Initially it seems he looked west, probably because he wanted to secure an alliance with the Frankish empire, but this initial outreach seems to have prompted the Byzantines to get nervous and attack the Bulgars in 864. The Bulgars were weak from a famine and surrendered to the Byzantines, and Boris was baptized by missionaries from Constantinople. When this news reached the Patriarch Photius, he sent a letter to Boris instructing him on how to be a proper orthodox Christian and informing him that he now fell under the jurisdiction of the Patriarch of Constantinople.

This arrangement, however, didn't sit well with the Bulgars, and Boris began to try and find a better deal. So, he turned again to the west, and initiated contact with Pope Nicholas I. His thought seemed to be that if he could play Rome and Constantinople off each other, he could secure the best situation for the infant Bulgar church and more significant autonomy from either side. Which brings us to the letter quoted at the beginning of this chapter. The Kahn Boris wrote a long list of questions to Pope Nicholas about the faith in 866 AD.

---

[3] J.B. Bury, *A History of the Eastern Roman Empire* (London: Macmillan and Co., 1912), 382.

Pope Nicholas responded, answering over one hundred questions, ranging from deeply theological questions about the law of God and the sacraments to trivial inquiries about when its lawful to bathe. And tucked into this massive question and answer letter is an inquiry about the legitimacy of wearing pants. It seems like the Bulgars were concerned; most Christians they had encountered did not wear pants regularly. Indeed, both western and eastern practices at the time derived from the more ancient Roman form of the toga, and trousers were fairly rare. For the Bulgars however both men and women wore long pants, made out of lighter material in the summer, and wool in the winter. Did conversion to Christianity require a conversion in clothing as well?

Saint Nicholas's response was no, your clothes don't really matter that much. It seems like he found this question amusing, writing that they must have asked this rather nonsensical question, "in [their] simplicity," because they "were afraid lest it be held against [them] as a sin, if [they] diverge in the slightest way from the custom of other Christians."[4] He writes that in general pants are worn by men rather than women, "but really do what you please. For whether you or your women wear or do not wear pants neither impedes your salvation nor leads to any increase of your virtue."[5] From there, the Pope moves to his more theological understanding of pants already quoted. "Spiritual pants" are the virtues that we put on to help us to live a temperate life and restrain

---

[4] Nicholas I, "Response."
[5] Ibid.

our disordered passions. These spiritual pants we should all wear at all times.

The relative importance of external things

What can we learn from this rather absurd episode? On the outset, the answer seems simple, Catholics can wear pants, and the Pope himself has declared it. However, I don't think most Christians lie awake at night wondering if their chosen way of dressing is permitted by the papacy. Rather, the value of this paragraph from an obscure ninth century letter comes from the fact that it reveals a little more deeply the relationship between the external, physical world, and the internal, spiritual one.

When we first come to know our faith, we, like the early Bulgarians, can think that the primary things of importance are external. To be a Catholic, I have to get ashes on Ash Wednesday, fast during Lent, and sit, stand and kneel a certain way at Mass or in prayer. It's natural, since we are physical beings, for us to think this way. Prayer when we are younger is primarily about memorizing certain phrases, correctly pronouncing words, and learning what to say and do in the liturgy since those are the things of religion which are most obvious and apparent to us.

As we grow older, our understanding must deepen. We begin to learn that the external aspects of our faith are there not for their own sake but to draw us deeper into the mystery, to spark within us a profound interior life. As physical beings, everything comes to us through our senses, and so in our weakness we need external things which in turn introduce us to the ineffable mystery of God.

This is why God became man in Jesus Christ, as the preface for Christmas Mass states, "so that, as we recognize in him God made visible, we may be caught up through him in love of things invisible."[6] And so we can see why Saint Nicholas doesn't really care one way or another about the Bulgars' choice of leg coverings—in the long run, it's not that big of a deal.

On the other hand, as Christians we do not progress *beyond* the physical. Our religion is sacramental, which means that spiritual realities are expressed in and through physical signs and symbols. In this world, you do not get to a point in the spiritual life where you don't need to participate the physical reality of Mass or Confession. The sacraments are the privileged ways God decided to convey grace, cognizant of our need for external signs as physical human beings. Those external channels of grace are necessary for our internal life to flourish.

Saint Thomas Aquinas wonderfully reflects on this state of affairs in his discussion of vocal prayer. He asks the question why should prayer be vocal when the person we are talking to, God, "knows the language of the heart"?[7] He responds that the physical act of speaking during prayer can help shape and excite the soul to a greater devotion, "because by means of external signs, whether of words or of deeds, the human mind is moved as regards apprehension, and consequently also as regards the affections." In other

---

[6] Preface I of the Nativity of the Lord, Roman Missal 3rd Edition, &c.

[7] Thomas Aquinas, *Summa Theologica*, Trans. Fathers of the English Dominican Province (Notre Dame: Christian Classics, 1948), II-II q. 83 a. 12.

words, being physical human beings, our spoken words shape our interior life.

Think of a concrete example: a relatively upbeat and optimistic person starts spending time with a more cynical crowd. To fit in, she tempers her naturally sunny disposition by repeating some of the more sardonic language of her peers, even though she doesn't really believe it. At first, not much changes, but gradually our optimist finds her thoughts and feelings begin to darken, and her natural personality changes. It's a reality that linguists and psychologists have studied for decades. The words we speak, the external situations we place ourselves in, shape our interior. Physical things matter because we as humans are an intimate union of body and soul. Our body affects our soul and vice versa—the two are deeply intertwined. Thus, in order to grow in internal goodness, we need to surround ourselves with external goodness.

This is why the Catholic Church is so full of external sensible things! It's been said before, but at Mass all our senses are engaged, the sound of the music, the beauty of the church building, the smell of the incense, the feeling of your knees as you kneel, and the taste of the accidents of bread and wine that you receive when you consume Christ's body and blood. All these things are meant to be sacramental (note the lower case 's'), in that they convey through their external symbolism and splendor some deeper spiritual truth. Pope Pius XII wrote concerning the liturgy,

> The worship rendered by the Church to God must be, in its entirety, interior as well as exterior. It is exterior because the nature of man as a composite of body and soul requires

it to be so… Every impulse of the human heart, besides, expresses itself naturally through the senses; and the worship of God, being the concern not merely of individuals but of the whole community of mankind, must therefore be social as well.[8]

It is not enough, however, for the worshiping Christian to remain at the level of the exterior. The Pope continues, "The chief element of divine worship must be interior."[9] We are called to worship God in spirit and in truth (John 4:23), drawn by external things into the deep interior relationship with the God who loves us.

Which brings us back to the specific context of Nicholas's teaching about trousers. In the long run, what type of clothing you wear is relatively unimportant. However, every aspect of our external, physical life should eventually point back and support the growth of our interior lives. When the external becomes too much of a concern, as it seems Nicholas thought in this case, then the attention needs to be drawn to the internal. This is the meaning of the strange digression into "spiritual pants" which represent the virtues of temperance and chastity. Nicholas desired to lead the Bulgarians to what is truly important, not the arbitrariness of a dress code, but rather growth in virtue.

So often in our spiritual lives we get hung up on the externals. We get caught up in what the music is for Mass, or what vestment

---

[8] Pius XII, *Mediator Dei*, no. 23.
[9] Ibid., 24.

the priest is wearing, or how people choose to receive communion. And while these things are not unimportant, if we fixate only on the externals, we miss the beauty of the mystery itself to which we are being drawn. This was the case for the ancient Israelites, who were too focused on the external rites of sacrifice without allowing those externals to shape their interior life. "For I desire steadfast love and not sacrifice, the knowledge of God rather than burnt offerings," (Hos 6:6) proclaims the prophet Hosea and likewise the Psalmist states,

> Not for your sacrifices do I rebuke you;
>> your burnt offerings are continually before me.
> I will not accept a bull from your house,
>> or goats from your folds.
> For every wild animal of the forest is mine,
>> the cattle on a thousand hills.
> I know all the birds of the air,
>> and all that moves in the field is mine.
>
> "If I were hungry, I would not tell you,
>> for the world and all that is in it is mine.
> Do I eat the flesh of bulls,
>> or drink the blood of goats?
> Offer to God a sacrifice of thanksgiving,
>> and pay your vows to the Most High.
> Call on me in the day of trouble;
>> I will deliver you, and you shall glorify me." (Ps 50:8-15)

Our Lord rebuked the Pharisees for similar reasons (See Matt 23:25 or 9:9-13), they were too caught up in the exterior, that they were unable to see the reasons for those exterior things. They mistook the external invitation for the actual wedding feast of the interior life and thus were unable to enter into the mystery of His love.

In this wonderfully strange episode of papal history, we see the whole drama of our human nature and its relationship with our spiritual God. God invites us to encounter him through external signs, and those physical, sacramental signs of his love lead us more deeply into the spiritual realities they signify. Even our sartorial choices can be instruments of his grace, can shape our hearts to greater self-denial and deeper love for God. And yet, we ought not get too caught up in external things to the detriment of the soul.

Taking Yourself Lightly

St. Nicholas's letter to the Bulgars does teach us one more thing about the spiritual life, that theological reflection does not have to be overly tendentious and grave. We have no evidence other than the letter itself, but I have to believe that the great pope in Rome, vested with the immense responsibility of the keys of St. Peter and the mandate to feed the flock of Christ, laughed when he wrote this response. It is too delightful not to do so. It reminds me of some of the more humorous questions that small children ask. To them the questions are very serious business indeed! But to the adult who hears them, they are the cause of tremendous mirth and authentic joy. And while the relationship between the physical and the spiritual in the Christian faith is important, its significance ought not dilute in anyway its humor.

There is a view of the faith, both in certain believers and in the secular world, that to be a believing Christian is to be stern. We must weep over the great injustices of the world and the magnitude of our sins. The stakes of eternal salvation or eternal damnation are too high for joking, aren't they? This mindset, however, is more rooted in pride than faith. We think that we are the ones responsible for our salvation and thus tremble at the thought of failure. The Christian recognizes however that this is not in truth the case. All is God's grace, he supports everything, and the only thing which keeps us from salvation is our own selfish pride. When God's love is tangibly present in our hearts and his grace evident in our lives, all our failures, and indeed all the things we took so seriously before, become causes of mirth. It's a much healthier spiritual practice to laugh at one's faults than to obsess over them. Yes, we should be sad that we turn away from God, but then we should laugh that we were dumb enough to think we wouldn't if we just tried harder. Laughing at yourself helps humble the soul and lighten the anxieties of life! All is not doom and gloom, waiting in nervous expectation for God's punishment and wrath – no, we have confidence in a God who bares our burdens, enabling our souls to be light! When the Lord did great things for the Israelites, the Psalmist tells us, "Then our mouth was filled with laughter, and our tongue with shouts of joy" (Psalm 126:2).

The saints were not all dour—they were in love! Lovers weep when they feel like they have betrayed their beloved yes, but they are filled with merriment at the mere thought of their beloved.

Falling in love with God brings freedom, not servitude, and even in the most important areas of life, there is intense joy, because God is present there. We as Catholics should be known not only by our commitment to Christ and the truth of the faith, but also in our joyful merriment. This truth is why St. Theresa of Avila famously exclaimed, "From silly devotions and sour-faced saints, good Lord, deliver us!" The great saints laughed for joy just as much if not more as they wept for their sins. As the great British author G.K. Chesterton famously wrote, "Angels can fly because they can take themselves lightly."

Chapter 2

St. Callixtus and the Meaning of Mercy

The Fall and Rise of St. Callixtus

You never know what you will find when you dig around in an ancient monastery's library. In 1842, a Greek scholar named Minöides Mynas was sent by the French government to the Orthodox Monastery at Mount Athos to search for interesting manuscripts. He discovered hidden away a forgotten text by St. Hippolytus of Rome, entitled *The Refutation of all Heresies*. The manuscript was thought to have been lost for centuries and once it was deciphered, it provided an incredible story about the life of one of our earliest popes, St. Callixtus I.

To properly tell this story, we have to begin with the author. As far as we can tell, Saint Hippolytus was an *antipope*, that is he was a priest who had himself declared Bishop of Rome in opposition to the legitimate pope at the time. He had serious disagreements with what he perceived to be heresy and laxity on the part of several popes in the early third century, and those disagreements lead him to break away from the Church at Rome all together and declare himself the true pope. The person against whom his anger was most forceful was a former slave named Callixtus. Naturally his account, while detailed, must be viewed with some suspicion. Indeed, most scholars describe it as particularly biased. Nonetheless, the story he tells is captivating!

Callixtus enters history as the slave of a Christian named Carpophorus who worked in the household of the emperor. Hippolytus relates that Carpophorus recognized Callixtus' talent and energy and as a young man set him up as his banker. Callixtus apparently failed at that task, losing the money his master had entrusted to him as well as the money of many pious Christians. Hippolytus says this was because of his own fraud and incompetence, but scholars say that economic circumstances of the time more than account for the failure. Regardless of the reason, Callixtus was distraught, he had failed. So, "Callixtus, perceiving these things, and suspecting danger from his master, escaped away by stealth, directing his flight towards the sea."[1] Arriving at the port close to Rome, Callixtus boarded a ship in the hopes of getting away from his master and starting a new life elsewhere, but before the ship could put to sea, the authorities appeared on shore. Seeing Carpophorus among them, "And knowing that himself would be inevitably captured, he became reckless of life; and, considering his affairs to be in a desperate condition, he proceeded to cast himself into the sea. But the sailors leaped into boats and drew him out, unwilling to come, while those on shore were raising a loud cry."[2]

The now captured Callixtus was told that he would have to repay the losses or else. He was a failure; he had let down not only his master but all those other Christians who put their trust and their money in his possession. He had tried to escape and had failed there, too, and like so many others in desperate circumstances he

---

[1] Hippolytus, *The Refutation of all Heresies,* https://www.new-advent.org/fathers/050109.htm Bk. IX, Cap 7.

[2] Ibid.

took drastic action. He ran into the local synagogue on the sabbath and caused a huge uproar, shouting out again and again that he was a Christian. It seems like his goal was some sort of martyrdom, hoping the that the Jewish members of the synagogue would put him to death themselves, or at least send him to the magistrate to do the job. Christianity was illegal at the time, and while a full-on persecution wasn't underway, if a Christian was caught, he or she would be punished accordingly.[3] The leaders of the synagogue dutifully brought the dejected Callixtus before the local magistrate and charged him with disrupting their peace on the sabbath. Carpophorus was called and testified that Callixtus wasn't really a Christian, he wasn't good enough for that name, and he was just a failure who lost his money. But after all this wild uproar and rushing all over Rome, the poor Callixtus was condemned to be sent to the Sardinian mines, a veritable death sentence.

But the story of course doesn't end there, because at that same moment the pope, Victor I, got a strange summons from the household of the emperor. Any call from the imperial household was something to cause anxiety, but for the head of an illegal sect to be summoned was particularly fraught. However, on his arrival Pope Victor discovered that he had nothing to fear. The note had come from the emperor's mistress Marcia, who was sympathetic to Christianity. She asked the pope if she could do anything for Christians who had been condemned to the mines. Overjoyed, Pope Victor gave her a list of Christians who had been sent there as pun-

---

[3] See letter of Pliny to Trajan, "Pliny and Trajan: Correspondence, c. 112 CE", *Fordham Ancient History Sourcebook*, https://sourcebooks.fordham.edu/ancient/pliny-trajan1.asp.

ishment, and Marcia agreed to have them released. Just as Callixtus arrived at the mines to serve out his punishment, by a shear miracle he received mercy from the emperor and returned to Rome.

His good luck did not end there. The pope himself had an eye to the wretched slave's rehabilitation. Pope Victor gave Callixtus a probationary assignment to keep an eye on him outside of Rome, but soon he was allowed to return to the city. Showing himself diligent and capable, Callixtus was eventually ordained a deacon by the Pope and placed him in charge of one of the major Christian cemeteries. You can still visit the catacombs of St. Callixtus to this day on the Appian Way in Rome. His diligence paid off, and he grew in the esteem of the local Church and the papacy, becoming a close advisor to the next pope, St. Zephyrinus. In time, this ex-slave and utter failure was himself elected the sixteenth successor of St. Peter, Pope Callixtus I.

Hippolytus's assessment of this fall from grace and subsequent rise to power is one of corrupt political machinations. Callixtus used his natural charm and powers to weasel his way into high office and to use the Pope as his puppet. He accused Callixtus of heresy, laxity in the practice of the faith, and personal immorality. Indeed, it was the election of Callixtus as pope that drove Hippolytus to openly oppose him as the antipope. In his book, Hippolytus portrays himself as the true Christian, opposing a corrupt and morally lax pope, whose history of moral and business failures ought to have more than disqualified him from serving as the Bishop of Rome. Hippolytus is on the side of those who really live the faith, who keep themselves above the base things of this world as Christ taught, and who maintain the fullness of religion. In this telling, Callixtus does not deserve the title of saint, he is a dark stain on the history of the early Church.

This is one way of reading the story, a corrupt former slave with an incredibly checkered past and a reputation for scandal works his way into high office for the sake of his own cynical gain. Were it not for Hippolytus' manifest animosity towards the pope, one could comfortably understand the history in this way without too much concern. There is, however, another way to see Callixtus' rise to power, and that is by looking at his story through the lens of mercy.[4] Judging someone's intentions in any circumstance is difficult enough, judging them seventeen centuries later with limited historical data is nearly impossible. But there are some clues which can help us see Callixtus in a less cynical light than Hippolytus's narrative.

To follow this thread, we must look at some of Hippolytus's critiques of Callixtus' papacy, specifically his treatment of those who had lapsed from the practice of Christianity. Hippolytus accused Callixtus of laxity for allowing those who had slipped in their practice of the faith, or even those who had turned away from Christianity all together, to return to the Church. Even some of the greatest of sinners were offered forgiveness, even though they had

---

[4] See for example Emanuela Prinzivalli, "Callisto I" in *Enciclopedia dei Papi,* https://www.treccani.it/enciclopedia/elenco-opere/Enciclopedia _dei_Papi. "La posizione callistiana è meditata teoricamente, ma proprio per l'intrinseca logica del suo discorso non richiede formalizzazioni, quanto piuttosto una prassi di misericordia, a maggior ragione in quanto l'oggetto della discussione pare incentrarsi da un lato sul peccato più praticato, cioè su quello di carattere sessuale, dall'altro su un nodo importante di politica ecclesiastica, l'atteggiamento verso i settari."

rejected the teachings of Christ for a time. Hippolytus accuses Callixtus of cynically offering mercy in order to gain popularity and power, while at the same time justifying his program scripturally. He writes,

> And in justification, he alleges that what has been spoken by the Apostle has been declared in reference to this person: *Who are you that judges another man's servant?* (Romans 14:4) But he asserted that likewise the parable of the tares is uttered in reference to this one: *Let the tares grow along with the wheat;* (Matthew 13:30) or, in other words, let those who in the Church are guilty of sin remain in it.[5]

In other words, Hippolytus saw Callixtus's attempts to bring forgiveness to lapsed Christians as shrewd political strategy—give the people what they want, mercy, and they will side with you no matter how corrupt you may be.

Accusations of laxity in the Church were not limited to this one situation; it was a common feature of early Christian disputes. Usually, these accusations would occur after a persecution, when those who had, out of fear of civil authorities, turned away from the faith, desired to return. Their sheepish entreaties for mercy would often be met by harsh words from those who hadn't fallen away, saying that they had lost their chance. The church father Tertullian, writing around the same time as Hippolytus, urged bishops

---

[5] Hippolytus, Bk IX, cap. 7.

to be severe and to not grant forgiveness too lightly.[6] In the middle of the third century, practitioners of the Novatian heresy asserted that anyone who had fallen away could not be readmitted to the Church, as did the Donatists heresy a century later. The emphasis was on the strictness of the faith; once one had been baptized, one had to remain faithful. Any fall was fatal. These rigorists have for centuries been condemned not merely as impractical or impolitic, but heretical. The popes again and again take the side of mercy, often, to be fair, with a lot of penance attached, but mercy, nonetheless. We see then that Hippolytus is not merely one harsh voice sounding out on its own, but he is also a part of a consistent trend in the Church which has been consistently rejected. Mercy is at the heart of what it means to be Christian.

With this in mind, we can read Callixtus' story very differently. Callixtus had a flawed youth, but it wasn't irreconcilable. In the Church, he had discovered the mercy of Jesus Christ, who knows all our sins and desires to heal us of our iniquities. The failures of his early life were forgiven, through the mercy of God working through the emperor, the pope, and the members of the Church who welcomed him back to communion. Callixtus received a second chance, and in knowing mercy himself desired to convey that mercy to others. His return to the Church in this reading is not based on cynical political manipulation but on genuine conversion, a reality which enabled him to see the goodness in others who had fallen themselves. While we can't know for sure if this was in

---

6 Tertullian, *On Modesty*, https://www.newadvent.org/fathers/0407.htm Some have speculated that Tertullian's call for severity may be aimed at Pope Callixtus directly!

Callixtus's heart, it's just as viable an explanation for his behavior as Hippolytus' screed, if not more so.

I desire mercy, not sacrifices

St. Callixtus shows us that mercy is truly the heart of what it means to be a Christian. As Pope Francis has written, "Mercy cannot become a mere parenthesis in the life of the Church; it constitutes her very existence, through which the profound truths of the Gospel are made manifest and tangible."[7] Christianity is not just about a set of beliefs, or about a moral code to be lived; it is a unique encounter with the triune God who gives each Christian abundantly from his treasure store of merciful love. We do not and we cannot earn that love; it is freely and gratuitously given.

The Church teaches that we can truly do nothing good without grace. In our fallen and sinful condition, we are unable to repent without God's grace working within us. Even our feeling of guilt which prompts us to return to confession is the product of *actual grace*, or the movement of God's love touching and drawing our hearts.[8] That movement draws us and gives us the strength to admit our sinfulness and to be forgiven, reestablishing the relationship of love that God desired for us from the beginning. But because of our fallen human nature, we cannot persevere in that love

---

[7] Pope Francis, Apostolic Letter *Misericordia et Misera* (Nov 20, 2019) https://www.vatican.va/content/francesco/en/apost_letters/documents/papa-francesco-lettera-ap_20161120_misericordia-et-misera.html

[8] See the *Catechism of the Catholic Church* (New York: Image Doubleday, 1997), nos 2000-2001.

until death without God's grace operating the entire time.[9] He is constantly at work, constantly calling, constantly strengthening, constantly drawing us back to Himself. We can truly do nothing without Him.

Grace, and thus mercy, is primary in every aspect of the spiritual life. It is not we who have chosen him, but he who chose us (John 15:16), and it is not that we have loved him, but "he first loved us" (1 John 4:19). In our weakness, in our brokenness, in our sinfulness, he chose us to be his adopted children. Indeed, as Gerald Manley Hopkins writes so eloquently, "Thou, thou, my Jesus, after me / Didst reach thine arms out dying... And thou couldst see me sinning."[10] We have done nothing to earn God's love; rather, we have rejected it so consistently, and yet in his tremendous mercy he never hesitates to call us home and welcome us back not only with open arms, but with great rejoicing.

Hippolytus' perspective is however an enticing one. It is so easy for us sinners to forget that we did not save ourselves. As we begin to live the Christian life, the temptation arises to think that this is all our effort. Sure, we give glory and thanksgiving to God, but in our hearts, we think, "I did this. Look how far I brought myself." Soon, like the Pharisee in the parable, we begin to look down on others with less strength and less resolve. I follow Christ, I go to Mass, I keep myself pure—they are sinners and are less than I. We are unable to be patient with those who are weak; we think that external purity and adherence to the moral code we have been taught

---

[9] *Catechism*, nos 2000-2001.

[10] Gerard Manley Hopkins, "O Deus, Ego Amo Te", https://poetry-nook.com/poem/o-deus-ego-amo-te

is the paragon of Christian perfection. But the Lord teaches us clearly: it was not the Pharisee who went home justified. It was the sinful tax collector, who in his humility, "would not even look up to heaven, but was beating his breast and saying, 'God, be merciful to me, a sinner!'" (Luke 18:13).

But what about the assertion that Hippolytus and so many others have made in the past, that mercy verges towards moral laxity and even moral relativism? Is he correct on that front? Can I just skate through life doing what I want, and God will have to take me in because he is merciful? It seems pretty easy to draw a line from "meeting people where they are" to "you're fine, I'm fine, who am I to tell you what is right and what's wrong." Aren't Christians called to "strive to enter the narrow way?" (Luke 13:24). Aren't Christians called to "shun immorality?" (1 Cor. 6:18). Hippolytus and others like him would seem to have a point; there must be a limit to mercy lest it turn to relativism.

To answer that objection, you must ask the question: what do I contribute to my own salvation? St. Augustine writes that "God does not save us without us," and likewise St. Paul tells us to "Work out your salvation with fear and trembling" (Phil 2:12). How are we saved? What do we as human beings contribute? The answer is a simple one—we try. Salvation is not dependent primarily on moral perfection; it's dependent on a will that is turned towards God. As one anonymous Carthusian monk writes, "All we need is good will and grace (which is God's good will): the two forces that make saints."[11] You can try and fail a million times in your life and be a saint; it's only when we stop trying that we truly fall away.

Consider two athletes, one for whom everything is natural and one who has to work very hard to succeed. If what you are looking for is success, of course you would select the one who is a natural. But if you are looking for heart, for someone who will give their all, you select the latter for your team, because you can judge, based on her work, that she cares more than the natural talent. God is not asking us for success; in fact, he knows we can't succeed on our own. Instead, he looks for our heart; that's what he desires, so we are called to try. When we fall down, when we sin, when we fail in big or small ways, how do we respond?

The most common way the devil attacks us in the moment after a fall is by pounding our soul with discouragement. We fail in some sin, big or small, and we start to beat ourselves up. I should be better than this! I thought I had conquered this fault! I should be making more progress! These are all responses of pride, we see ourselves in a Hippolytan light, holding ourselves to high standards that implicitly we believe we have to achieve on our own. When we fail, we want to reject ourselves just as Hippolytus rejected the sinful in Rome. We become impatient with our own progress because we don't want to admit to ourselves that we are weak, that we fail, that we are sinners. Often, we think that to be a saint it means to no longer be a sinner, but if we listen to the greatest saints, they usually are the ones to proclaim that they are the greatest sinners.

---

[11] Anonymous Carthusian, *They Speak by Silences* (Hertfordshire: Gracewing Publishing, 2006), 87.

When we understand the primacy of God's mercy, our image of God changes. We no longer see in God merely a stern and unrelenting judge as Hippolytus does. God is a judge, the Bible tells us so, but he does not, "hold you over the pit of hell, much as one holds a spider, or some loathsome insect over the fire, abhors you, and is dreadfully provoked:" as one 18th century preacher described him.[12] Rather, he is like the parent watching his child learn how to walk. We, the spiritual toddlers, take halting shaky steps and then immediately fall. And like a little child, we cry and are frustrated at our inability to do what seems simple. But the father isn't frustrated! The father doesn't expect his toddler to run a marathon or even to walk across the room. The father doesn't say, "You worthless child, I'm done with you. You can't even walk!" No, the parents of that little toddler are so excited at even the smallest sign of progress, even the smallest desire to walk. They never tire of picking the child back up, putting them on their feet, and encouraging them endlessly to try again! It's only we, the spiritual toddlers, who become discouraged and frustrated because we can't walk swiftly.

In order to truly understand and practice mercy, we have to be willing to admit to ourselves our own sinfulness. The doctor can only truly heal when the patient admits there is something wrong; so, too, we can only truly receive mercy, when we accept and acknowledge our own failings. As Fr. Jacques Phillipe writes, "What often blocks the action of God's grace in our lives is less our

---

[12] Jonathan Edwards, *Sinners in the Hands of an Angry God.* https://www.jonathan-edwards.org/Sinners.pdf

sins or failings, than it is our failure to accept our own weakness."[13] We don't like to see ourselves as sinners, we want to see ourselves as saints, and so we begin to think of ourselves as better than we are. When we then subsequently fall, in our pride and self-centeredness, we berate ourselves. In reality, it is not through effort or force of will that we will triumph. It's only through being patient with our weaknesses and humbly turning again to the Lord that true growth in the spiritual life occurs. God's grace is operative if only we return to him as best we can, just as St. Callixtus did. To strive to enter the narrow gate does not mean achieved moral perfection; it means recognizing our weakness and giving *even that* to God, and trying our best to love Him with our whole hearts.

Mercy and Evangelization

Mercy is essential not only for our own growth in the spiritual life, but also for evangelization. Hippolytus mocks those who flocked to St. Callixtus as irreverent and lax, not worthy of being called Catholics. And yet the number of those who came to St. Callixtus grew precisely because they found mercy. Even Hippolytus admits this, writing, "And many persons were gratified with his regulation, as being stricken in conscience, and at the same time having been rejected by numerous sects; while also some of them, in accordance with our condemnatory sentence, had been by us

---

[13] Jacques Phillipe, *Interior Freedom* (New York: Scepter Publishing, 2017), 33.

forcibly ejected from the Church."[14] Mercy is essential for successful evangelization. If preaching the Gospel is merely the calling of
people to a higher way of life, it will fail. Those called might be inspired, they may desire to live a more profound and spiritual life,
but they won't know how to understand their weaknesses. Eventually, they will come to see Christianity as external adherence to a
strict code of conduct, rather than as a profound transformation. If
instead one leads with mercy, accepting people where they are and
helping them to know that they are loved infinitely and eternally by
the God who knows all their sins, there is room for true conversion.

This doesn't mean ignoring sin and not preaching the truth. It
doesn't mean saying to someone, "It doesn't matter how you live so
long as you are a good person." There are so many difficult situations people find themselves in, struggling with same sex attraction, expressing disagreements and trauma from bad experiences
with the Church, or having a checkered past like St. Callixtus's.
Mercy doesn't mean whitewashing over difficulties. A doctor can't
really be said to be caring for a patient if she isn't willing to give the
patient the difficult news. But a heart which is merciful also recognizes that we need to meet people where they are. St. Thomas
Aquinas says in many places, "Everything is received according to
the mode of the receiver."[15] In other words, people can only hear
the truth if they are able to receive it. Evangelization requires understanding the challenges and struggles of another and not judg-

---

[14] Hippolytus, bk IX, cap. 7.
[15] See for example, Summa Theologiae, 1a, q. 75, a. 5; 3a, q. 5.

ing them for their sins, but rather loving them as God does. "Love one another as I have loved you" (John 13:34), Jesus admonishes his apostles. God knows all our sins and yet chooses to love us completely, giving us every chance to change, and never giving up on us. The merciful person recognizes the sinfulness of others and calls them to a new life in grace, but also recognizes that true evangelization requires a love which is unconditional. It requires the love of Christ.

You Cannot Give What you do not Have

St. Callixtus was able to show mercy because he had been shown mercy himself. He knew he was unworthy of the office to which he had been called. He knew that he had failed multiple times, but that in that failure he was still loved and redeemed by Christ. That openness to grace enabled him to be a channel of grace for others: to evangelize through mercy. He had been loved so gratuitously, and he knew that the only response to such profound compassion is to "love the Lord your God with all your heart, and with all your soul, and with all your mind..." and to "love your neighbor as yourself" (Matt 22:37,39). If we are to show mercy to others, if we are to evangelize others, we need to recognize how undeservedly loved we are. We need to accept our failings and the fact that we will fail again in the future, knowing that his "power is made perfect in weakness" (2 Cor 12:9). To do so opens our hearts to understand the height and depth of His love for us (Eph 3:18), which is not based on what we have earned but purely on his gratuitous mercy. St. Callixtus understood this love and allowed it to grow in his heart. This deep love culminated in his own martyrdom, when in the midst of an anti-Christian riot he was thrown out of his house window in Trastevere on October 12, 222 AD.[16] He was a true sinner, who through God's mercy became a saint.

---

[16] Prinzivalli, "Callisto I".

Chapter 3

St. Martin I Disappears

The Invisible Pope

In 652 AD, Pope Martin I celebrated an important Mass at the great Papal Basilica of Santa Maria Maggiore (St. Mary Major). The importance of this Mass didn't have to do with the liturgical season or a special anniversary. Rather, this Mass was the first step towards a reconciliation with the Byzantine Emperor Constans II in Constantinople. The emperor and the pope had been in conflict over a particular point of doctrine, a conflict which had only grown throughout Martin's papacy. But today, at Santa Maria Maggiore, there would be a move towards healing the rift. The Byzantine chamberlain Olympius, who had come to Rome to try and push the pope to accept the emperor's side, had had a change of heart, and now wanted to be reconciled to the Roman Church and receive Holy Communion at Mass.

As Pope Martin processed into the already ancient church, he walked past pictures from the Old Testament and towards the massive mosaiced back wall of the basilica, what is today a triumphal arch placed above the high altar. The wall was covered in scenes from the life of Mary, the Mother of God, depicted dressed in the splendid garments of a Roman Empress. Sitting at the top of the arch was a small dedication, "Xystus Episcopus Plebi Dei," Sixtus the Bishop to the people of God. The entire wall was commissioned centuries before Pope Martin by his predecessor, Sixtus III, as a celebration of the successful resolution of another doctrinal dispute. Factions in the east had said it was improper to call Mary the *Theotokos* or "God Bearer". Resolution of this older conflict had come at the Council of Ephesus in 451 AD, when it was officially proclaimed that Mary is indeed the "God Bearer" and those who believed otherwise were not only incorrect, but they were also heretical. Out of joy and love for Mary, Pope Sixtus commissioned the renovation and decoration of this beautiful Basilica in her honor.

Pope Martin might have thought a similar joyful resolution was beginning in his dispute with the emperor. Olympius, the representative of Constans II, was in the congregation, ready to receive communion and thus unite himself, and by extension the emperor, back into a relationship with the Pope. But what Pope Martin didn't know was that the whole event was a sham. Olympius never intended reconciliation, but seemed to have been sent to Rome with the instructions to get the Pope to yield to the emperor's way of thinking by any means necessary.[1] His plan was to murder the Pope in cold blood, there at Mass. He had told one of his servants to station himself nearby, and when the Pope came down from the altar to give Olympius communion, he was to stab the Pope.[2] But when the moment came and Olympius was ready to receive communion, his servant didn't make a move. After Mass, Olympius

[1] Horace Mann, *Lives of the Popes in the Middle Ages* (London: Kegan Paul, Trench, Trubner, 1925), Vol I, 392.
[2] *The Book of Pontiffs (Liber Pontificalis)*, Raymond Davis ed. (Liverpool: Liverpool University Press, 1989), 68.

questioned him thoroughly—why hadn't he struck as planned? The servant responded that just when he was about to strike, he could no longer see the Pope at all! The Pope had disappeared from his vision completely. A chronicler from the time wrote, "But almighty God, who casts a shield around his orthodox servants and delivers them from every evil, blinded the exarch's spatharius [servant]…"[3]

Olympius, we can suppose, was initially skeptical of his servant's story. But the servant swore on oath before several others that he was unable to see the Pope at all, and that was what prevented him from killing Martin I as planned.[4] As the realization of what had happened gradually began to sink into Olympius, he began to fear. He recognized that his battle wasn't just against a powerful man, but against God himself. Only God could have made this incredible thing come to pass to save his servant Pope Martin. Olympius came to understand the reality of St. Paul's great boast in the *Letter to the Romans*, "If God is for us, who is against us?" (Rom 8:31). It truly is folly to try and fight against heaven itself, and that realization brought Olympius to a true conversion. He confessed to the Pope his scheme and told him everything that he had planned and what had happened at the Mass. He decided at once to abandon his emperor's instructions and serve the Church by taking his army and defending southern Italy from an invasion by Saracen raiders, where he died in 653.

This story is only a part of a series of fights between the Emperor Constans II and Pope Martin I. After Constans heard about

---

[3] *The Book of Pontiffs*, 68.
[4] Ibid., 68

what happened to Olympius, he was furious. In a fit of rage, he had Pope Martin arrested and brought across the sea to Constantinople to force him to give into his theological demands. Martin suffered greatly, was found guilty of high treason, and was sentenced to exile in March of 655, where he died a few months later. What was the dispute that had so enraged the Byzantine emperor, and which caused such violent actions against the Pope?

What's all the fighting about?

The question at hand was about the internal nature of Jesus Christ and had its roots in the conflict settled in the time of Pope Sixtus III two centuries earlier. At that time, various factions in the Church fought over the title of Mary, whether or not she could be called the God-bearer. And while on the surface the fight seems to be about the Mother of God, in reality it was about Jesus Christ himself. The opponents to the title (called the Nestorians) said that you couldn't legitimately call Mary the God-bearer because she only gave birth to the human nature of Jesus, God doesn't have a mother because he is eternal. As God, he was never born, and thus Mary couldn't be called his mother. In effect, the Nestorians separated the human nature and the divine nature of Jesus too much. The response of the Church was that the divine and human natures are so intimately united in Jesus Christ that you can coherently say that Mary is the Mother of God. The Council of Ephesus declared, "The divine nature and the human nature formed one Lord and

Christ and Son for us, through a marvelous and mystical concurrence in unity."[5]

As often happens with doctrinal disputes, the defeat of one side of the argument prompted an overcorrection on the other side. While before the Nestorians overly separated the human and divine natures in Christ, now a faction overly unified them. This faction asserted that there aren't separate divine and human natures in Christ, but only one nature, the nature of the Word of God. From this position they received their name, the Monophysites, from the words *mono,* meaning one, and *physis,* meaning nature. After years of contention between the various parties, the Church addressed these issues at the Council of Chalcedon in 451 AD, declaring that the faith professed,

> ...the same Christ only begotten Son, our Lord, acknowledged in two natures, without mingling, without change, indivisibly, undividedly, the distinction of the natures nowhere removed on account of the union but rather the peculiarity of each nature being kept, and uniting in one person and substance, not divided or separated into two persons, but one and the same Son only begotten God Word, the Lord Jesus Christ...[6]

---

[5] Henry Denzinger, *The Sources of Catholic Dogma* (Fitzwilliam, NH: Loreto Publications, 2007), no. 111, p. 49.

[6] Ibid., no. 148, p. 61.

The decree of the Council of Chalcedon was accepted by most of the Church and is still the heart of the Church's understanding of who Jesus is to this day.

But not everyone accepted Chalcedon. In the east, especially modern-day Iraq, and in the south, Egypt and Ethiopia, monophysites still held sway. Which brings us to the controversy in which Martin I was embroiled. In contrast to our relatively pluralistic societies today, in which many religions can interact and exist legally, the emperors of the ancient world saw a multiplicity of religious practice within their domains as an evil to be avoided. An empire needed the cohesion that a single faith provided in order to face the challenges presented by the world outside their boundaries. So, time and again we hear in history of an emperor who just wants to put doctrinal fights behind him, regardless of the outcome, in order to get everyone on the same page. Who really cares about the subtle distinctions that priests fight over? Can't we all just get along?

The split between the orthodox and monophysite Christians was a thorn in the side of numerous Byzantine emperors, a thorn that more enterprising rulers attempted to remove through clever theological ideas. One such emperor was Heraclius, who in 638 AD attempted to unite the monophysites and orthodox with a new proposal: Jesus had two natures, but only one energy or will.[7] The new position has come to be called *Monothelitism*, from the words *mono*, for one and *thelema*, will. It seemed like a logical compro-

---

[7] Aidan Nichols, *Rome and the Eastern Churches* (San Francisco, Ignatius Press, 2010), 216.

mise which would enable both sides to come together to support a single understanding of the nature of Christ, but the compromise position was not successful in bridging the gap. There was still conflict and division within the Church, and the dream of one empire and one faith seemed further off than ever. So, the next emperor, Constans II, thought, if we can't get on the same page, then we should avoid the subject completely. He issued a note which has come down to us through history as the *Typos*, requiring that no one in the empire preach or discuss the question of whether Jesus has one will or two. Like a family dinner at Thanksgiving, if you can't agree on politics or religion, just don't talk about them at all.

The Pope, however, refused. The job of the papacy is to teach the truth of the faith and to combat error, to be the firm foundation of doctrinal certainty upon which the Church is built. And this conflict with Constans II led to the attempted murder of Pope Martin and his being dragged off to Constantinople in chains. After slogging through all that history of seemingly obscure fights over apparently trivial points of theology, the question immediately becomes apparent: what's the big deal? Is the question of whether Jesus has one will or two wills really worth all this trouble, not to mention violence? The *Typos* of Constans II seems entirely reasonable; if you can't agree, agree to disagree and do not fight about it.

The Importance of the Truth

The answer to that question gets to the heart of the Christian faith and the role of the papacy within the Church. Far from being a strange story about a disappearing bishop and a trivial point of contention, the conflict over monothelitism and Martin I's insistence that he teach the truth points to something deeper. It requires us to inquire into the nature of truth itself, and the reason why Jesus came to earth in the first place.

While philosophers have disputed it for centuries, truth is essentially the relationship between what I think and what is real. How accurately does what is in my mind reflect what is objectively present? An easy way to think of this is in the realm of science. I have a theory about how some molecule will react in certain circumstances. I test that theory through a series of experiments, and gradually I determine if that theory is true. Does it correspond to the results of my tests? If the experiments show something different than my theory, like a good scientist I have to change my theory and account for the unexpected results. My theory is true if it was proven correct, and it is false if it was proven incorrect.

One might think, "That's all fine and well for science, but the faith is something much more subjective. It's about my experience, my spirituality, my own search for goodness and peace, areas of thought and of life that seem inherently subjective." But in the Christian faith, that is not entirely true. Christianity is about a relationship with a person, with God himself, who became man in order to communicate his inner nature to us. "And this is eternal life, that they may know you, the only true God, and Jesus Christ whom you have sent" (John 17:3), the Lord says in the Gospel of St. John. Christianity is a revealed religion; God tells us the truth about Himself. It is not merely a collection of myths that we tell ourselves to make sure we are good people. The truth, and believing the truth, is essential to being a Christian.

The early teaching of the Apostles and Church Fathers emphasized the importance of believing true doctrine. St. Paul was constantly on the watch for people who preached alternatives to the truth. He tells the Galatians, "But even if we or an angel from heaven should proclaim to you a gospel contrary to what we proclaimed to you, let that one be accursed!" (Gal 1:8). Likewise, we hear in the Acts of the Apostles that the early disciples Priscilla and Aquilla take the preacher Apollos aside to correct him on points of doctrine (Acts 18:26). Finally, St. John emphasizes that you can tell those who are antichrist by the fact that they do not acknowledge that Jesus has come in the flesh (1 John 4:3).

Again, however the question arises, why is this so important? Can't we, as Thomas Jefferson famously did, take the moral teachings of the Bible and leave the doctrinal details and just be good people? Why fight over controversies of the inner nature of God and the relationship of the human and divine in Jesus Christ? The Church's response, fundamentally, is that you need to know someone in order to have a relationship with him or her. Take a simple example. If I met someone for the first time who said he or she was friends with my sister, I would of course be happy to chat with that person. But if through the course of the conversation I came to realize that they thought my sister was a 6'4" Romanian shot-putter with a side hustle as a street performer in Bucharest (which she decidedly is not), I would be skeptical about whether the person was actually friends with her. How could that person be if his or her understanding of my sister is so antithetical to who she actually is? If I pressed the issue and the person responded, "Well your sister *to me* is a Romanian athlete," I could say in response, "That's all well and good, but it's not my sister. You clearly have an imaginary friend and not a real one."

Friendship and love require truth. When you meet someone you want to be friends with or even for whom you are feeling the initial stirrings of love, you want to get to know that person more. What is his or her favorite band? Where is he or she from? What's his or her family like? What's his or her favorite flavor of ice cream? By knowing that person truly, you are able to love that person truly. And nothing is worse for a relationship than a false idea of who the person actually is. The trope of the lover being deluded by rose tinted glasses into ignoring the reality of the beloved is basically a proverb. At some point in a relationship, for love to grow the beloved can't just be a projection or an ideal in the mind; he or she has to be a real person that the lover encounters truthfully.

Which brings us to Christ. If we are saved through a relationship with Jesus Christ in his Mystical Body the Church, the truth is essential. Jesus is a real person, indeed more real than a family member, friend, or celebrity you see on social media. And if he is a real person, we can say things that are true about him and things that are false. We can say that he is good, and loving, and fully man and fully God. These things are true, they correspond to reality, and the more we know them, the more we love him. We can't say that he is just a man, or that he is cynical, or that he is an ancient alien. We don't believe these, not because some old priests arbitrarily told us we couldn't believe them, but because they don't correspond to reality, and we can't encounter Jesus truthfully if we believe he is what he is not. The truth leads us into relationship with a real, powerful, and eternally loving person: God himself who became one of us! Falsehood prevents us from entering fully into that relationship.

Mystery and Understanding

The question still remains: why pick a fight over such a seemingly trivial detail about Jesus? If the Byzantine emperor was denying that Jesus was good or loving that would be one thing—but whether or not he has one will or two, does that really matter? And aren't there aspects of the intimate life of God that are really too esoteric or inaccessible for theologians that they really shouldn't be arguing about them in the first place? The attempt of theologians to enter the truly obscure and incomprehensible inner nature of God himself seems to be vain at best. Viewed in this light, it is more appropriate to approach the inner mysteries of God with a reverential silence than to fight over strange dogmas at an international level. The silence imposed by the *Typos* would still seem to make sense: the mystery of God is beyond us and must remain that way.

The reality of Jesus as a person helps us respond to this line of argument as well. Every person is a mystery. If I were to try and tell you about a good friend of mine, I could list all sorts of qualities. I could give physical details, eye color, hair color, height, shoe size. I could tell you his history or his personality traits, where he was born, where he studied, his favorite music, his quirks. I could show you a picture, or a video on my phone. All those things would be true, but they wouldn't exhaust the reality of my friend. A person is greater than his or her description—there is a great mystery pre-

sent which can't possibly be fully expressed, even with an exhaus-
tive description. The friendship touches a deeper level which is real
even if it can't be defined.

The mystery of the inner life of Jesus is the same. Our attempts
to describe him, to tell people about Him, to understand exactly
who he is, can't possibly exhaust the mystery of his inner nature.
All the words of scripture and all the teachings of the tradition of
the Church are totally inadequate at exhausting that mystery. And
yet just like my attempts to describe my friend, they are not false.
They do touch the reality of the person, even if they don't exhaust
him. Even though I can't wrap my mind fully around the mystery
of my friend, that doesn't mean I throw up my hands and say nothing. Like so many mysteries of the human experience—beauty,
truth, love—we attempt to describe even though we know that the
description is inadequate. Every poet knows that his or her words,
however appropriate, fail to do justice to the reality they approach.
Every lover knows that his or her praise of the beloved is so paltry
compared to the real object of their affection. Every true theologian
knows that his or her formulae and definitions are only rushed
sketches of an incomparable beauty briefly glimpsed.[8] And yet
knowing that, the poet seeks to write more, the lover can't stop
praising his or her beloved, and the theologian seeks to understand
more deeply the mystery of God.

Mystery transcends our ability to comprehend, but it doesn't
mean that our attempts to understand are pointless. When we pon-

---

[8] St. Thomas on the feast of St. Nicholas famously had a vision compared with which all his great theological work appeared as "such straw."

der the mystery, it begins to take possession of our minds and hearts. As St. Thomas writes, "It is impossible for any created intellect to comprehend God; yet 'for the mind to attain to God in some degree is great beatitude,' as Augustine says."[9] We are more closely united to the object of our knowledge and enter into true communion with the God who is "the truth" (John 14:6). The attempt to understand the inner nature of Christ, then, is not fruitless. Theologians understand that it is inadequate, but it does touch the reality of God in some small way. And for that reason, it is important that it be true. St. Martin I defended the truth of Jesus's two complete natures because it is vitally important that we understand who he really is. He is fully God, and thus fully able to free us from our sins and raise us up through adoption into the intimacy of his family. And he is fully man, able to sympathize with our weakness and communicate to us in our own language the realities of divine love. Jesus indeed is the first person to try to tell us about the inner nature of the Trinity, knowing of course that the human words he used to enlighten us couldn't do justice to the fullness of the truth; nevertheless, he revealed to us the Father, and sent the Spirit into our hearts to "guide you into all the truth" (John 16:13).

As part of his own self-revelation of "the mystery that has been hidden throughout the ages and generations" (Col 1:26), Jesus gave us a way to be certain that we are authentically encountering Him in truth: he established the Church, His own mystical body. The rock upon which that Church was built was the confession of St. Peter, and from the earliest moments the whole world has looked

---

[9] *ST*, I, q. 13, a. 7.

to the faith of Peter and his successors, the bishops of Rome, as the *regula fide*, the rule of faith, to help us to know what is true about Christ. As early as the 2nd century, St. Irenaeus wrote, "For it is a matter of necessity that every Church should agree with this Church [the church of Rome], on account of its preeminent authority."[10] St. Peter is like the close friend or brother of someone we desire to know. He can tell you, "Yeah, that's what he is like, or no, that isn't him." And through history the Popes have played the role of safeguarding the knowledge and proclamation of the truth that help us to come to know Jesus Christ. Hence the intense pressure placed on St. Martin by Constans II to acquiesce to his decrees. Constans knew how essential St. Martin was to the faith of the Church universal—if he was not on board, the emperor's plans would never be legitimate. St. Martin, however, knew the person of Christ better, and he couldn't say something was true that was false, or refuse to say what was true about Jesus.

That insight is the heart of the whole story. Faith is not just a philosophy or just a moral code; it's an encounter with a real objective person. It is the place where we meet God himself, incarnate in Jesus Christ and dwelling in our hearts in the Holy Spirit. He isn't the product of our imagination, nor does he conform to what we want Him to be, anymore than any person conforms to what we want. He is a real person, and though his inner nature is mysterious, by entering that mystery we find a friend whose divine nature raises us to glory.

---

[10] Irenaeus of Lyon, *Against Heresies*, Bk. III, Ch. 3, no. 2.

This is the truth that Olympius realized when his servant miraculously couldn't see the object of his violent intentions. He realized that this wasn't a political intrigue or a clash of cultures or philosophies. He realized that he was attempting to fight a person—and more than a person, God himself. He understood, albeit through strange circumstances, the reality that each Christian eventually comes to grasp; that God is real. And meeting that real God, the God of power and might, but also love and forgiveness, the God who "so loved the world that he gave his only Son, so that everyone who believes in him may not perish but may have eternal life" (John 3:16), his heart was changed. While we might not meet God in the same way as Olympius, it must be part of our life of faith as well, to follow the truths of the catechism which we are taught into an encounter with the real and living God Himself.

Chapter 4

Pope Sylvester II and the Giant Abacus

A Mathematician Pope

"The Church is anti-science." This stereotype, heard constantly in our society, stems especially from an Enlightenment era campaign to paint the Church as at best superstitious—at worst, a manipulator of the ignorant. The great philosophe Voltaire was perhaps one of the most forceful opponents of the Church. He is supposed to have said, "You will notice that in all disputes between Christians since the birth of the Church, Rome has always favored the doctrine which most completely subjugated the human mind and annihilated reason." The age of faith, following the decline of the Roman Empire and before the great reawakening of the Renaissance was for these thinkers, and indeed for most people today, an age of darkness.[1]

Holders of that modern consensus would be shocked to be standing in the nave of the Rheims Cathedral in the late 10th century. While not the towering Gothic Cathedral that is so famous today, the earlier and still impressive Romanesque church was the site of intricate mathematical experiments, previously unknown to the medieval west. If you found your way into that Church, you

---

[1] Note that one of the first people to use the term "Dark Ages" was the Church Historian Cardinal Baronius. The Church herself acknowledges that times were difficult!

would have seen several students rushing around moving markers throughout the large nave of the cathedral, responding to calls floating down from high up in the clerestory. Looking up, you would see a very animated and yet thoughtful monk, directing the movements below. The church had been turned into a massive abacus, a calculation device from the ancient world, and the monk was the local math genius, Gerbert of Aurillac, the future Pope Sylvester II.

The word genius is thrown around lightly today, but in the case of Gerbert of Aurillac it is well deserved. Gerbert was raised in southern France and educated as a young monk at the monastery in Aurillac. When he was still a young man, his talent for learning was recognized and a local noble brought him to Spain where he studied mathematics. Spain at that time was divided between the territory of the Muslim Umayyad Caliphate in the south and the Christian Visigoth kingdoms in the north. The Umayyad civilization then well-outpaced the Christian world in terms of learning. At a time when a European library containing a hundred books was considered extensive, the library of Abdur Rahman III in Cordova boasted nearly 400,000.[2] Arabic mathematics were particularly advanced, due in part to the use of Arabic numerals which were more suited to advanced calculations than the Roman numerals still in use in much of Europe. While he most likely didn't make it all the way to Cordova, Gerbert unpacked the mathematical and scientific treasures he found in Spain and brought them back with him to Christian Europe in 970 AD.

---

[2] Mann, *Lives of the Popes,* Vol. V, 13.

His return brought him into the higher spheres of European society at the time. He found himself in Rome and his obvious intelligence and extensive learning caught the eye of Pope John XIII. The pope wrote to the Holy Roman Emperor, Otto I, telling him about this educated young monk and recommending him to serve as the imperial tutor.[3] By 973, he was teaching at the cathedral school at Rheims, not only on mathematics, but also on philosophy, poetry, logic, music, and astronomy.[4] He pursued truth wherever he could find it, either in the texts of Arabic manuscripts, ancient Greek and Roman poetry, or the classical works of the philosophers Boethius and Aristotle. He introduced Arabic numerals to Europe as well as the abacus and the astrolabe, an instrument used to understand the motions of the stars. He was also a prodigious collector of books and sought out rare texts from across Europe for the cathedral school. In the middle of the darkest part of the dark ages, Gerbert was a true light of learning. After a somewhat tumultuous career as an abbot and then Archbishop, he was chosen to be the Pope and was installed in the Chair of St. Peter on Palm Sunday, 999 AD, taking the name Sylvester II.

---

[3] Richer of Saint-Remi, *Histories*, Vol II, Ed. Justin Lake, Cambridge, Harvard University Press, 2011, 65.

[4] As one chronicler from the time described his study, "There is no necessity to speak of his progress in the lawful sciences of arithmetic and astronomy, music and geometry, which he imbibed so thoroughly as to show they were beneath his talents, and which, with great perseverance, he revived in Gaul, where they had for a long time been wholly obsolete." William of Malmsbury, *Chronicle of the Kings of England*, Trans. J.A. Giles (London: Henry G. Bohn, 1847), 173.

As pope, Gerbert did not stop his pursuit of learning, and while managing the affairs of the Church and corresponding with the Holy Roman Emperor about political matters, he was still writing to learned friends and colleagues about particular solutions to geometrical problems or about books that he had found. He promoted learning just as assiduously as he had as a humble monk, including the study of Arabic and of mathematics taken from Muslim or pagan sources. While Pope Sylvester died in 1003, the foundation he laid both in his teaching career and through his papacy were the seeds which would flower into the great medieval universities of a few centuries later.

Contrary to the modern expectation to find nothing but darkness in the Church at the turn of the first millennium, Pope Sylvester II appears as a polyglot and scholar, a promoter of the pursuit of truth who was not only celebrated by the Church but who rose to the Chair of St. Peter. He gives the lie to the belief that the dark ages were merely a time of superstition and ignorance, that adherence to dogma and doctrine prevent the flourishing of scientific inquiry. That does not mean that there wasn't superstition; indeed, Pope Sylvester himself has been slandered by superstitious historians. The eleventh century English chronicler William of Malmesbury accounted for the learned pope's abilities as the product of a pagan education which taught him "the art of calling up spirits from hell." He describes Gerbert as having made a bargain with the devil, who would speak to him through a possessed statue that would direct him while pope. Ironically, William himself recognizes that his attribution of demonic power to the Pope because of his learning is itself a common trope in history. He writes,

"Probably some may regard all this as a fiction, because the vulgar are used to undermine the fame of scholars, saying that the man who excels in any admirable science, holds converse with the devil."[5] And yet he concludes that from his research he cannot dismiss his "belief of [the pope's] with the devil."[6]

The Church and Science

Gerbert of Aurillac's life and studies show that the Church, despite individual examples throughout the centuries, is not dogmatically opposed to scientific research or secular learning. Indeed, it has promoted scientific study through the millennia. Pope Sylvester is just one of many monks, priests, or religious sisters who have contributed significantly to scientific research. Alongside Gerbert of Aurillac, mention could be made of St. Hildegard of Bingen, Gregor Mendel, Nicholas Copernicus, and Georges Lemaître, to name a few deeply religious men and women who also were recognized for their pursuit of scientific study. And yet there are those moments in history in which the Church or members of the hierarchy did not seem as inclined to promote new learning. The case of Galileo, of course, comes to mind immediately. It can appear at a cursory glance that there were times in which the truth of the faith seemed separate from the truth of science, if not contradictory. How can a Church support scientific truth in such a case? Are there two separate truths, one spiritual and one secular?

---

[5] William of Malmesbury, *Chronicle*, 174.
[6] Ibid.

Truth, as discussed in a previous chapter, is the connection between reality and the mind. Something is true if it reflects reality itself. It's a logical absurdity to say that something can be true and false at the same time and in the same respect, so one can't believe something to be true scientifically while false in the realm of faith. Truth is one, because reality is one, so faith can't logically be opposed to the truths revealed in science and vice versa. As Pope John Paul II writes, "The two modes of knowledge lead to truth in all its fullness. The unity of truth is a fundamental premise of human reasoning..."[7] The mathematician who pursues the truth through the understanding of numbers is not in any way contradictory to the theologian who pursues the truth in the realm of revelation—indeed they are each seeking aspects of the one truth which underlies all reality, God Himself. Again, to quote the great Pope John Paul II, "There is thus no reason for competition of any kind between reason and faith: each contains the other, and each has its own scope for action."[8]

Gerbert himself had to grapple with the relationship between the sciences in his own career. In 980 AD, he was challenged by another learned man at the time, Otric of Saxony, to a debate over the division of knowledge. The debate hinged on the proper relationships between the sciences, in this case the subordination of mathematics to physics. Gerbert boldly declared in front of a crowded auditorium, and the Holy Roman Emperor himself, that, "mathe-

---

[7] John Paul II, *Fides et Ratio*, https://www.vatican.va/content/john-paul-ii/en/encyclicals/documents/hf_jp-ii_enc_14091998_fides-et-ratio.html, 34.

[8] Ibid., 17.

matics, physics, and theology are all coequal species of the same genus, in which they participate equally."[9] To sort through the more esoteric scholastic language, Gerbert stated that all branches of knowledge are ordered towards the same end, the pursuit of the truth. And yet at the same time they are divided and pursue that truth through different methodologies.

The apparent conflict between science and faith comes from the failure to acknowledge that each way of knowing has its own realm of expertise. Modern proponents of the supremacy of science assert that basically all we can know we know through the scientific method, and they seek to cast doubt on or reject any knowledge that arises by a different discipline.[10] The argument in favor of this viewpoint is usually based on the incredible success the scientific method has had in improving human life—for example, the great advances in technology or medicine or our understanding of the natural world. The scientist asserts that in the past, what we acknowledged as the work of God, or the gods, has now been shown by science to have natural understandable causes. For these reasons, we ought to throw out the other forms of knowledge, which don't seem to offer us much if anything in the way of true progress.

This argument was put forward most forcefully in the seventeenth century by the French philosopher Rene Descartes. Frus-

---

[9] Richer, 95.

[10] John Paul II, *Fides et Ratio*, 88. "This is the philosophical notion which refuses to admit the validity of forms of knowledge other than those of the positive sciences; and it relegates religious, theological, ethical and aesthetic knowledge to the realm of mere fantasy."

trated with the apparent failures of the more traditional medieval philosophy and theology, and enticed by his studies in mathematics, Descartes wondered if he could come to an understanding of all knowledge through a mathematical method. He resolved to "sweep wholly away" all philosophical learning and traditional knowledge and attempt to rebuild human wisdom from scratch, using mathematical principles and searching for clear and concise ideas.[11]

The error in this scientific understanding is that it is fundamentally hypocritical at its roots. When science says that it is the only way to know things, it is making a claim which is not based on the scientific method. That claim is no longer science; it is verging into the realm of philosophy, which science has just calmly asserted is not to be trusted and should be replaced by science. It is logically incoherent and falls apart. Science can do a lot, but there are realms of human knowledge which are beyond its capacity and are valuable in their own right.

Modern science is one particular way of looking at the truth, but it is not the only one. It's like looking at a beautiful landscape at sunset. You can take in the landscape in a variety of ways. You can use your eyes and naturally take in its colors and its beauty and observe the characteristics of the world through natural light. But that isn't the only way to look at it. You could buy an infrared camera and see a different wavelength of the light and notice things that you couldn't see with the naked eye. You could use a spectrometer and learn about the various elements which make up the scene

---

[11] See Rene Descartes, *Discourse on Method*, Part II.

around you. Just because with your natural sight you can only see a certain portion of the spectrum of light doesn't mean that you are seeing everything there is to see.

Science doesn't have the capacity to see the full spectrum of human knowledge. There are certain fundamental and important questions it doesn't have the ability to answer. Science can answer the question how; it has a much harder time answering the question why or Who. The scientific method can be used to understand how atoms come together and how they can be broken apart and release terrifying amounts of energy, but it can't answer the question of how that incredible power *should* be used, if at all. Science can tell us how the world was made, but it can't tell us *why* and *by Whom* the universe was made and what its purpose is. These questions are outside the scope of scientific inquiry, and the conflict among faith, philosophy, and science lies in each branch of knowledge attempting to answer the questions of the others. Saying that the only knowable or worthwhile truths are those that are observable and empirical is like saying that the only thing worth knowing about a painting is the material composition of its pigments. Whatever science might say in such a situation, there is a depth of meaning found in a painting or a symphony or a novel which is fathomless to the strict scientist.

Unscientific Superstition?

If the Church is so supportive of scientific and mathematical inquiry as demonstrated by Pope Sylvester, what can explain the many examples of the stodgy conservatism and superstitious dogmatism which are so easily caricatured by opponents of the faith? First and foremost, it has to be remembered that the Church is both a divine and a human institution, and that members of the Church are sinful. One of the consequences of sin is ignorance of the truth. After the original fall from grace, human nature was "wounded in the natural powers proper to it, subject to ignorance, suffering and the dominion of death, and inclined to sin."[12]

The darkness and ignorance into which human nature has been plunged because of sin naturally breed superstition and a hesitance towards new ideas. It is challenging to maintain an open mind that is able to judge impartially what is true and what is false; human beings are naturally inclined towards only pursuing truth within a certain sphere of comfort or which is involved in pleasure. If we stake our claim on something being true, our own pride and ego will often prevent us from being open to a new idea which is contrary to our opinion. Likewise, our intellect's ability to discern what is true can be dulled by addictions to worldly pleasures and sinful habits.[13] I would rather cling to what makes me comfortable than to have an uncomfortable or unexpected truth forced upon me. Being fully open to wherever the truth leads requires humility and a trust in truth itself, which is a challenge for any human being, much more a person caught in sin. Many occasions of opposition to scientific progress in the Church's history can be attributed to this cause.

---

[12] *Catechism*, no. 405.

[13] See for example St. Thomas Aquinas *ST* II-II, q. 15.

Sinfulness likewise prevents proper communion and communication among the various elements of humanity. It breaks the bonds of solidarity and introduces conflict into the human family. This is the main lesson of the biblical story of the Tower of Babel. The sinful pride of humanity shattered the original communion of society which was manifested through the multiplication of languages and the inability for humans to understand one another. Even if one has the best of intentions, it can be hard to truly understand someone else. That inability is exacerbated when two people are formed in dissimilar or even opposed ways of thinking. In many cases, the conflict between faith and reason comes about because scientists and theologians lack the ability to speak to one another. As Pope St. John Paul II noted the Galileo case was, "a tragic mutual misunderstanding that has been interpreted as a reflection of a fundamental opposition between science and faith."[14]

St. Thomas Aquinas's wonderful phrase "everything is received according to the mode of the receiver" speaks to this truth. In order for one to engage intellectually with someone else, one has to be able to have the mode to receive what the other is saying. For example, a strict psychologist, who has been raised and formed in a post-modern scientific education, is not able to be open to the Thomistic description of the powers of the soul. It all sounds like pseudoscientific mumbo jumbo. Likewise, a theologian's eyes might glaze over when hearing about the beauty of the phospholipid bilayer of the cell or the intricacies of quantum mechanical cal-

---

[14] John Paul II, "Discourse to the Pontifical Academy of Sciences", https://www.vatican.va/content/john-paul-ii/it/speeches/1992/october/documents/hf_jp-ii_spe_19921031_accademia-scienze.html, 10.

culations. They are seen as boring or unimportant not out of a lack of appreciation for these things but out of a lack of vocabulary to understand. Modern education is the result of a long process of separating and specializing disciplines to such an extent that communication among any given fields is nearly impossible. It is natural that in such circumstances theology and science would come into conflict—they don't have the words or the conceptual frameworks to understand one another.

Finally, there is another explanation for the conflict between science and faith which has less to do with sin and more to do with the nature of the Church herself. The Church is a *traditional* organization. Tradition in this sense means more than a mere passing down of customs and stories; it means a connection to a living reality from which the Church receives her life. God revealed himself to the world in Jesus Christ, telling us about his inner life and inviting us into a relationship with him. He then commissioned his apostles to invite more into that inner relationship. That commission to preach entails a content, Christ himself. As St. Paul succinctly describes his commission, "For I decided to know nothing among you except Jesus Christ, and him crucified" (1 Cor. 2:2). The fathers of the Second Vatican Council described this traditional aspect of the Church as enabling the faithful to enter a relationship with the Word Himself. They write, "This sacred Tradition, then, and the sacred Scripture of both testaments are like a mirror, in which the Church, during its pilgrim journey here on earth, contemplates God, from whom she receives everything, until such time as she is brought to see him face to face as he really is (cf. 1 Jn. 3:2)."[15]

The Church as an institution is naturally protective of this treasure of tradition, and thus is inherently conservative and wary of blindly endorsing new ideas. She meditates and ponders on each new way of thinking to see if it is in accord with the tradition given by Christ through the Apostles or if it's a deviation from it. So, when science comes along and states that one way of thinking which has been seemingly valid for centuries is no longer acceptable, the Church is naturally hesitant to get on the scientific bandwagon. Temperamentally, she does not rush to conclusions lest by dashing off after one intellectual fad, she mistakenly abandons the connection to Christ inherent in the tradition.

Similarly, the Church spends time pondering the implications of new discoveries on human nature and human flourishing. She takes the time to answer the moral questions that science cannot, and will often put the brakes on scientific progress in the name of preserving human dignity. For example, as scientists rush ahead with new advancements in gene editing which may have a multitude of positive outcomes, the Church urges scientists to slow their progress in order to consider the ethical results of changing fundamental aspects of human nature. Sometimes, this means saying that an avenue of research must be considered completely off limits as being morally abhorrent, and in such a case the Church points to the truth that there is a greater good than mere technological

---

[15] Second Vatican Council, *Dei Verbum*, in *Vatican Council II Vol. 1: The Conciliar and Postconciliar Documents*, ed. Austin Flannery (Northport: Costello Publishing Company, 1998), 7.

progress: the growth and flourishing of the soul. This does not mean that the Church rejects advancement, but rather that, like a good gardener, she helps to prune and direct intellectual growth for the good of humanity. Checks on intellectual innovation are not always signs of superstitious repression—more often than not, they are merely the results of prudence.

A Catholic's View of Science

The proud claims of science can cause fear in the hearts of believers. What if science does disprove faith? What if they are right in claiming to be the totality of all knowledge and God is shown definitively to be a human delusion? Such fear can motivate Christians to reflexively close the door to scientific inquiry and even to difficult questions an unbeliever might pose. Someone once asked me if it was sinful to question the Church too much. You might be inclined to think, yes, just believe and don't question. Such an attitude betrays a lack of faith in the reality of truth. If Christians are certain that all truth comes from God and leads to God, no question made in good faith can undermine belief. Christians ought to be confident in the fundamental reality of God and see every question, even if tinged with cynicism or made in an aggressive tone, as reflecting in some part a deep desire to know what is true.

Such confidence derives fundamentally from encountering the living God. As we meet God in faith and allow him to enter our hearts in charity, we meet reality Himself, truth Himself, and we love Him. No question or scientific challenge can shake the certitude of one who is in love. This certitude is not the surety of a delusion that ignores the incongruous or harsh realities of existence through emotional fantasies. It is rather the certitude of someone who has seen through even the most difficult parts of life and has met the author of them all. Nothing can truly shake this foundation of faith because it is rooted in reality itself, and that reality is one. Such an encounter gives us the firmness of knowing the truth of God and knowing that all legitimate scientific inquiry is part of that truth. The Catholic is open to all questions because all questions point to the truth of God.

The Catholic, however, must recognize that just as science needs to give way to theology in the realm of the immaterial, science has its own legitimate claims to supremacy in the realm of observation. Not all conflicts between faith and science occur because of the overzealousness of scientists. There are also occasions in which theologians overstep their bounds. For example, overly literalistic ways of reading the Bible can lead to situations in which theologians veer into the realm of science, claiming the world to be thousands instead of billions of years old. Theologians have to understand and value the role of scientists who seek truth using their own particular methods and disciplines, which fundamentally point to the same truth, just in a different way. In the end there can be no contradiction between the two, no holding of two distinct and conflicting truths. The believer can be confident in the truth revealed by God and in the truth discovered through the scientific method.

With such a foundation, the Christian should welcome scientific pursuits as enthusiastically as Gerbert of Aurillac. All truth leads to God in some way, and the pursuit of knowledge in its many pathways will only enrich the human experience. There is nothing to fear from legitimate experimentation and questioning because behind all natural puzzles is the hand of God at work, and at the root of every sincere question is the spark of divinity which desires that we come to know. Pope Sylvester II was truly a light in a dark age, and his exuberant love of mathematics and natural philosophy laid the groundwork for the great flourishing of intellectual life in the 13th century.

Chapter 5

St. Sergius I and the Lamb of God

Another Imperial Tussle

Just before receiving communion, Catholics say at every Mass, "Lamb of God, who takes away the sins of the world, have mercy on us." We can recognize in that oft repeated phrase the exclamation of St. John the Baptist, who pointed out Jesus to his disciples as the "Lamb of God who takes away the sin of the world!" (John 1:29). And while we say it again and again, to the point that it might seem a merely banal repetition of a stock religious phrase, the origin of the *Agnus Dei* in the Roman liturgy is found in a period of intense theological conflict between Rome and the Byzantine Empire.

The drama of emperors and popes did not cease with the death of St. Martin I, whom we discussed in a previous chapter. A new struggle began in the 7th century as the Emperor Justinian II wanted to assert his control over the church and let to what is known to history as the Quinisext Council. The Quinisext Council was a meeting of almost entirely Eastern bishops in Constantinople in 692 AD. While the stated purpose of the council was to rectify omissions of the fifth and sixth ecumenical councils (hence the name Quinisext, from the Latin words for fifth and sixth), in reality it was called as part of an attempt by the emperor to enhance his legacy.[1] His namesake, the great emperor Justinian I had called a council, the Second Council of Constantinople, so if he, too, was going to be a great emperor, he also needed a council to his name.

The Quinisext council was primarily disciplinary in nature, and it laid out over one hundred canons regarding how Christians, clergy and laity, should act. Several of those canons took direct shots at the practices of the Roman Church, including clerical celibacy and the use of unleavened bread for the Eucharist. One of these canons took issue with the practice of depicting Jesus as the Lamb of God. It stated,

> In order therefore that that which is perfect may be delineated to the eyes of all, at least in colored expression, we decree that the figure in human form of the Lamb who takes away the sin of the world, Christ our God, be henceforth exhibited in images, instead of the ancient lamb, so that all may understand by means of it the depths of the humiliation of the Word of God...[2]

To translate the rather archaic language into more modern terms, the council did not approve of images representing Jesus as a lamb because that imagery was imperfect compared to displaying

---

[1] Constance Head, *Justinian II of Byzantium* (Madison: University of Wisconsin Press, 1972), 65.

[2] "The Canons of the Council in Trullo often called the Quinisext Council" in *the Nicene and Post-Nicene Fathers*, 2nd series, Vol XIV edition by H.R. Percival, 401.

him as a man. It thus banned those images outright and directed the church universal to do the same.

The decrees of the Quinisext council were sent to Rome to Pope Sergius I, who, needless to say, was not happy with their directions. When the official acts of the council arrived in Rome, the Pope did not "tolerate those copies to be received or opened for reading. Instead, he rejected them and set them aside as invalid, choosing to die sooner than consent to erroneous novelties."[3] Pope Sergius would not even let the ambassadors from Constantinople officially present the results of the council. It was a step which was not taken lightly. Pope Sergius must have thought about his many predecessors who had been forced into a conflict with the Byzantine Empire—those fights did not always end well. Pope Sergius' political situation was not much different than that of his predecessors, the Byzantine Empire still had a lot of military and coercive power, and an ambitious emperor on the world stage would not let a hang up over Church discipline get in the way of his prestige. The conflict escalated, with the Byzantine emperor sending his servants to try and force the Pope to sign the acts of the council and the Pope refusing to budge.

While this story of courage and faith in the face of secular opposition is inspiring, what separates it from other stories of the same sort is one final note in Pope Sergius's biography. The entry in the *Liber Pontificalis* (Book of Popes) for Pope Sergius states, "He laid it down that at the time of the breaking of the Lord's body the clergy and people should sing, 'Lamb of God, who takest away

---

[3] *Book of Pontiffs*, 82.

the sins of the world, have mercy on us.'"[4] The singing of the *Agnus Dei* during the breaking of the bread was a feature of the liturgy in Syria and the Levant, and Sergius who was Syrian by heritage, would have had exposure to that particular tradition.[5] When he became Pope, he added the *Agnus Dei* to the Roman celebration of Mass, and it remains to this day.

While there isn't a direct causal link in the historical record, it's hard not to connect this insertion into the liturgy with the conflict Sergius had with the Byzantine emperor. The emperor outlaws the depiction of Christ as the lamb of God, and Sergius counters by inserting the chanting of the *Agnus Dei* into the Roman liturgy. If that were the case, it would be one of the most enduring thumbings of the nose in history. For lack of a better term, a papal "trolling" of the Byzantine Emperor is in some way responsible for our daily supplications to the Lamb of God. Regardless of the motive and the historical connection, it is abundantly clear that St. Sergius had a devotion to the image of Christ as the Lamb of God, a devotion which was rooted in scripture and history, and which helps Christians understand the role of Jesus in our salvation.

---

[4] Ibid, 84.

[5] Joseph A. Jungmann, *The Mass of the Roman Rite*, Vol. 2 (New York: Benzinger Bros. 1955), 334. Jungmann acknowledges that there is some debate regarding the actual introduction of the *Agnus Dei* by Sergius, but he does concede that it most probably did enter the Rome rite at this time with the influx of Syrian refugees fleeing the armies of Islam.

The Wedding Feast of the Lamb

The scriptural use of the imagery of the Lamb of God is rooted in the ancient sacrifices of the Temple. The spotless unblemished lamb was mandated to be used at the Passover sacrifice, representing for the Jewish people their own offering to God of themselves. The Lord instructs Moses in the Book of Exodus, "Your lamb shall be without blemish, a year-old male; you may take it from the sheep or from the goats. You shall keep it until the fourteenth day of this month; then the whole assembled congregation of Israel shall slaughter it at twilight" (Ex 12:5-6). They gave the best of their flocks because they wanted to externally show God that they were giving their hearts. Yet the sacrifices of Israel were not effective; they did not bring about the true forgiveness of sins (see Heb. 10:4). They were awaiting a new sacrifice, a perfect sacrifice, the true and spotless lamb.

When John the Baptist proclaimed to the people by the Jordan, "Here is the Lamb of God who takes away the sin of the world!" (John 1:29), he was speaking to this ancient reality. Jesus would be the new lamb, the spotless lamb, whose sacrifice would truly bring about forgiveness of sins. And as St. John tells us, he was sacrificed on the Cross while the Jewish priests were sacrificing the Passover lambs at the temple. As Pope Benedict XVI writes, the early Christians, "recognized Jesus as the true Lamb, that in this way they came to see the true meaning of the ritual of the lambs... he gave them himself as the true Lamb and thereby instituted *his* Passover."[6]

The image of the Lamb of God was popular in the early Church because it specifically called to mind and taught the reality of Christ's sacrifice. Jesus offered Himself as the one perfect sacrifice on the altar of the cross. For the same reason Catholic Churches today feature prominently the crucifix, a tangible reminder of the depth of the Lord's passion and of His love. Yet there is an objection frequently made to this reminder, one that may be behind the Quinisext Council's decree forbidding the depiction of Christ as a lamb. The objection is today often made that Christ rose; he triumphed! Why ought we wallow in the melancholy reality of his suffering when he rose from the dead and is victorious over sin and death? Isn't it just a medieval morbid fascination with pain and suffering?

Behind this objection is a deeper theological root, a certain lack of comfort with the idea that Christ was a sacrifice at all. How could a loving God demand in obedience such an act? Was God a bloodthirsty tyrant, whose anger with the sin of humanity needed to be appeased with the most dramatic and painful of deaths? This doesn't seem to be the God of love! Why would God desire this act by his Son? Why, too, would he want us his faithful to stay in this moment—why not instead focus on the joy and glory of the resurrection?

---

[6] Pope Benedict XVI, *Jesus of Nazareth,* Vol. 2 (San Francisco: Ignatius Press, 2011), 112-113.

As he is wont to do, Saint Thomas Aquinas answers this question quite beautifully. He asked the question, "What is it about the death of Christ that redeemed humanity? Was it primarily the magnitude of his sufferings?" His answer was that though suffering played a role, it wasn't the primary role. Humanity's sin could only be expiated by being atoned for. We had broken a relationship of infinite love, and in our human weakness were unable to properly repair that relationship of love. To atone for our actions, a new act of perfect love had to be made, which is what Christ did on the cross. Thus, St. Thomas writes, "But by suffering out of love and obedience, Christ gave more to God than was required to compensate for the offense of the whole human race. First of all, because of the exceeding charity from which He suffered…"[7] It wasn't suffering *per se* that God demanded, but love.

Yet the question remains, why the cross? Why the sacrifice? Christ had to atone for humanity's waywardness in a human way. It wasn't enough for him to love God divinely; he became a man to love God on behalf of all of humanity, and thus reestablished the relationship of love between each person and God. He needed to speak to God in a human language, and the deepest human love language is sacrifice. Jesus himself says it in the Gospel, "No one has greater love than this, to lay down one's life for one's friends" (John 15:13). On the Cross, Jesus said to God and to each of us: this is how greatly you are loved. God-made-man was willing to lay down his tremendous dignity, to suffer, to be abandoned, to be mocked, and to be killed in order to make the perfect act of love.

---

[7] St. Thomas Aquinas, *ST* III, q. 48, a. 2.

When we look at the Crucifix or hear the words at Mass, "Lamb of God...," we should not merely focus on the pain and sacrifice; we should see, beneath the pain, the love. We can understand that love better because it was demonstrated to us in a way we can understand. Christ used human words and human actions to convey the immensity of His divine love.

The cross is not an imposition, a pure punishment by an angry God. It is a willing sacrifice of love, an expression of love which is immediately recognizable to any human lover. The human lover goes to extraordinary lengths to please his beloved: he buys her flowers or does menial tasks for her, not because she requires it as payment but because he needs in some way to express his love. G.K. Chesterton beautifully makes this point when talking about St. Francis of Assisi's love of fasting. He writes,

> Men will ask what selfish sort of woman it must have been who ruthlessly exacted tribute in the form of flowers, or what an avaricious creature she can have been to demand solid gold in the form of a ring; just as they ask what cruel kind of God can have demanded sacrifice and self-denial. They will have lost the clue to all that lovers have meant by love; and will not understand that it was because the thing was not demanded that it was done.[8]

---

[8] Chesterton, *St. Francis of Assisi*, 91-92.

Jesus is the Lamb of God, not because he is placating a ruthless and harsh judge, but because he is consumed by love—and like every lover, he must express it.

There is no adequate way for human beings to perfectly describe love. We turn to poetry because prose falls short; we turn towards music because normal unadorned words don't do justice to the gravity of love. A husband cannot express directly the totality of his love for his wife. He cannot connect their hearts by a spiritual cable and download directly the entirety of his affection. For humans, it is only through outward signs that we glimpse the reality of love's depth. The Lord expressed in his sacrifice a love deeper and more immense than any human love, the love that is God's very nature, and he did so by offering himself, body, blood, soul, and divinity as a gift of obedience to his Father.

The Image of the Father

The Quinisext Council's prohibition of figurative images of Christ was really the first phase in a broader conflict about the use of images themselves. A generation later a Byzantine Emperor banned all images of Jesus and the saints completely in what we today call the iconoclast heresy. The logic of the two ecclesiastical crises is the same. In the case of St. Sergius, the emperor decreed that images that depicted Jesus in a figurative way were imperfect representations and had to give way to only images of Christ himself as a man. The iconoclasts took that conclusion and moved a step further: any image at all is inadequate in depicting God and thus any religious icon had to go. To use icons in prayer was superstition and idolatry since the glory of God cannot be contained in a physical depiction.

The problem with this logic is that it is directly contrary to Jesus's very nature. Jesus Christ is the physical, "image of the invisible God, the firstborn of all creation" (Col 1:15). God knew that his love could only be expressed properly to humanity through physical means, and so the Second Person of the Trinity, the divine Word of God, became incarnate. In becoming man, he made tangible the intangible nature of God's love. In taking on our human flesh, he was able to use human imagery to describe the indescribable realities of the Trinity. One of St. Sergius's own deacons, Pope Gregory II was Pope at this time, and he responded forcefully to the iconoclasts, "He gave to us His Holy Body, and made us to drink His Precious Blood, in the Mystical Supper; then, as it were, He washed our feet, and we eat and drank together with Him, and our hands handled Him, and He made Himself known to us."[9]

Images are given to us in our weakness, to draw us by way of them to understand part a deeper truth. When a teacher starts to teach math to young children, he or she doesn't begin with esoteric concepts of numbers and equations. A second grader can't conceptualize pure mathematics. Rather, the teacher makes the vague concepts concrete, using blocks or fingers or any number of visual aids to help the young students begin to understand the more abstract concepts. Likewise, God, the perfect teacher, knowing humanity's own lack of conceptual ability, chose to teach us at our

---

[9] "Gregory II Letter to Emperor Leo" in *the Seventh General Council*, trans. John Mendham (London: William Painter, 1850), iv.

own level. The image of the Lamb of God, or any image used in devotional life, is there to speak to us on our human level so that eventually we might adhere more closely to the infinite.

Catholics reverence images not because of what they are per se, but because of what they communicate. A mosaic of the Lamb of God is still just a collection of tiles. Tiles are not able to save us from our sins. But because in the tiles we enter more deeply into the knowledge and love of God, we honor them. The Second Council of Nicaea, which definitively rebuked the iconoclastic heresy, puts it this way, "For the honor of the image passes to the original'; and he who shows reverence to the image, shows reverence to the substance of Him depicted in it."[10] Seeing the image of the Lamb of God in our churches and having the words "Lamb of God" regularly on our lips at Mass draw us closer into a relationship with the God who gave himself up for us, as a living image of the eternal love of God.

An Act of Mercy

Whether or not St. Sergius I adjusted the Roman liturgy to troll the Byzantine emperor, the entire conflict over the Quinisext council could seem to be overly harsh and vindictive. Yet when we hear the strange coda of the story, the compassionate side of St. Sergius is revealed. Justinian II was furious at the Pope's defiance and sent his servants to punish Sergius for his obstinacy. The serv-

---

[10] Council of Nicaea II, in *The Sources of Catholic Dogma*, ed. Henry Denzinger, no. 302, pg. 121.

ants of the emperor arrested and extradited several of the top offi-
cials in the papal administration, and then they turned their eyes
on the Pope himself. The chief servant of the emperor, the *spatharius* Zacharias, was told to arrest the Pope and bring him back to
Constantinople to face charges.[11] But when Zacharias arrived at
Rome, he discovered that the people of Italy were not on the Byzantines' side. A large crowd of soldiers and common folk from
around northern Italy marched on Rome to prevent the Pope's ex-
tradition, and they arrived at the city just after Zacharias. Discover-
ing that he was surrounded, and afraid that the mob would lynch
him, Zacharias ran to the Pope, and forced his way into St. Sergius's bedroom. The Pope's biographer describes the scene, "In
tears he begged the pontiff to have mercy on him and not let anyone take his life."[12]

In the meantime, the pro-papal mob found their way into the
city and surrounded the Lateran Basilica where the Pope lived,
threatening to break into the palace if Zacharias was not brought
out to them immediately. Hearing the roar of the mob outside and
realizing he was completely helpless, Zacharias got down on his
hands and knees, crawled under Pope Sergius's bed, and "went out
of his mind and lost his senses."[13] How the tables had turned! The
proud and ruthless servant of an ambitious and domineering emperor was crying like a child and hiding under the Pope's bed begging for help. The Pope, in his turn, consoled the weeping soldier

---

[11] *Book of Pontiffs*, 82.
[12] Ibid.
[13] Ibid.

and himself went out to the crowd to beg for mercy for his erst-while enemy. Taking his seat at the entrance to the Lateran, he calmed the crowd outside. Their fury dissipated and the Pope made them promise only to return Zacharias to Constantinople and not to kill him outright. At the same time, back in Constanti-nople, the emperor himself was deposed in a coup and the pressure on the Papacy was alleviated.

If the way God made known his divine love was through the sacrifice of the Lamb of God, the fathomless depth of that love was plumbed by Jesus's calling out, "Father, forgive them, they do not know what they are doing" (Luke 23:34). He died to show even those who were nailing his hands and piercing his side that they were loved. In loving his own enemy, St. Sergius became an icon of God's mercy, clearly manifesting to the Church and the world that the sacrifice of the Lamb of God was made for all.

Chapter 6

Benedict IX, The "Grover Cleveland" of the Papacy

One Pope, Three Separate Terms

How many men have been Pope? It seems like a simple question, and the simple answer most people will tell you is 266. During the election of Pope Francis in 2013, news anchors regularly prefaced their reporting of the Cardinals' gathering at the conclave as choosing the 266th pontiff. Even the official list of Popes in the Vatican's *Annuario Pontifico* numbers Pope Francis as number 266. Yet, if you go back and count, there are only 264 men who have held the keys of St. Peter. Why? Benedict IX.

Benedict IX was born in the middle of the 11th century as Theophylactus, the son of the *de facto* dictator of Rome Alberic II. He was born into what historians call the dark ages of the papacy, a time when popes were chosen by political rulers from their own families in order to secure secular political objectives. Alberic II had done a surprisingly decent job of choosing popes up until this point, but with his son Theophylactus he made a big mistake. He was the spoiled child of an autocratic ruler and was most likely in his late teenage years or early twenties when he was chosen.[1] Histo-

---

[1] Horace Mann, *Lives of the Popes...*, Vol. V, 240 See also Ovidio Capitani, "Benedetto IX," in *Enciclopedia dei Papi*, https://treccani.it/enciclopedia/benedetto-ix_%28Enciclopedia-dei-Papi%29/. Some chroniclers at the time stated he was as young as 12 years old at the time of his

ry is replete with examples of young, privileged teenagers gaining power at an early age, and almost uniformly it does not end well.

Benedict IX was a disaster as a pope, and everyone knew it. He added to infamous sexual immorality a ruthlessness in his governing the people of Rome. The Church historian Horace Mann writes, "we are told in most general terms that he was unceasingly occupied in plundering, murdering, and otherwise oppressing the Roman people."[2] After being driven out of Rome at least once before, in 1044, the people of Rome had had enough and in an armed revolution threw him out and elected a new pope, Sylvester III.

Now this is where things get tricky. Some historians recognize Sylvester III as an authentic pope, while others call him an anti-pope. His time in Rome was brief, only a couple of months in 1045, and he was elected while Benedict IX was still claiming to be pope himself. The *Annuario Pontifico* mentioned above throws up its hands during this period and says we aren't really sure who was and who wasn't a legitimate pope since the canon law at the time was not very clear on the subject.[3] It includes Sylvester III on the list of Popes as does most posters and lists of Popes that you can find. In 1045, Benedict IX returned to Rome, kicked out Sylvester, and established himself once again as pope, and like the American president Grover Cleveland, started a second, noncontiguous term in the Chair of Peter.

---

coronation as Pope, but most modern scholars think a date of 20 to 25 years to be more accurate.

  [2] Mann, 248.

  [3] *Annuario Pontifico,*

The craziest part of Benedict IX's story, however, is yet to come, because he vacated the papacy for a second time, this time without any doubt of his intentions. Shortly after returning to Rome from his first exile and starting his "second term" as pope, Benedict IX resigned the papacy. From our current historical distance and due to a lot of particularly scandal-mongering chroniclers who despised Benedict IX, it's difficult to say exactly why things took the turn they did. But it does appear that Benedict IX realized that he didn't really want to be pope anymore. On top of that, he seems to have become enamored with a cousin and sought her hand in marriage.[4] Her father, of course, was taken aback completely and said that the marriage could only go through if he resigned the papacy.

Faced with such a difficult decision, Benedict IX turned to an old spiritual advisor: his godfather, the archpriest John Gratian. Fr. Gratian was known to be an upright and holy man. He was a priest who, at a time when most monks and priests were totally disregarding their promises of celibacy and prayer, was well regarded for his piety and chastity. Benedict turned to his spiritual father and presented the choices in front of him. He could remain pope and not get married and continue the lifestyle he had been living, or he could abdicate the papacy, get married, and have the burdens of office removed from him. John, being a good priest and knowing that Benedict was a very bad pope, advised his godson that he should absolutely resign the papacy. It would be a blessing for the

---

[4] Mann, 250-251.

whole Church and remove a stain of scandal. But then Benedict IX dropped the other shoe: he needed money.

Benedict IX had become accustomed to a certain style of life as both the son of a secular ruler and now the pope, and if he was going to leave it all and get married, he would need some cash on hand to continue his lifestyle. So, he told Fr. Gratian that he would need a sizable amount of money in order for this to work. John Gratian apparently thought that this was a small price to pay to restore some dignity and holiness to the papacy, so he gave Benedict the cash he wanted. Benedict left town, and John Gratian himself was elected Pope and took the name Gregory VI.

It seemed like this was a step in the right direction for the papacy to have removed such a terrible pope. St. Peter Damian, the great reforming monk of the 11th century, wrote an effulgent letter to the new Pope Gregory VI, pouring on the praise in paragraph after paragraph,

> I give thanks to Christ, the King of Kings, most reverent lord, that I who am aflame with thirst to hear nothing but good things of the apostolic see, should now in the company of many well-wishers drink a generous toast to your great deeds. To be sure, the imbibing of such sweet news has restored my mental digestion so that my spirit within rejoices and my tongue straightway proclaims this song of

praise: 'Glory to God in the highest heaven and on earth peace to men of good will.'[5]

Finally, a reform-minded and holy priest had been named pope, and those who celebrated reform initially were enthusiastic.

St. Peter Damian's letter, however, mentioned the seeds of Gregory's downfall and the beginning of the "third term" of Benedict IX. After all the biblical imagery describing how great this moment was, St. Peter noted that finally the practice of *simony* could be stamped out. He writes, "Let trafficking in this wicked business be ended, let the counterfeiting Simon now quit his minting of money in the Church."[6] Simony takes its name from the character Simon the magician in the Acts of the Apostles, who tried to buy the power of the Holy Spirit from the Apostles (see Acts 8:9-24). The practice was one which was common in the church of the 9th through the 11th centuries and involved the buying and selling of church offices. If you had a son whom you wanted to be a bishop, you paid the right price, and he would get the job.

Now the problem is pretty apparent: the way Pope Gregory VI got his position looks an awful lot like simony. He forked out a lot of cash to the hapless pope in order to convince him to resign and was then elected pope himself. The initial enthusiasm experienced by some in the Church at the prospect of a reformer becoming pope turned quickly to disgust at how he was elected. On top of

---

[5] St. Peter Damian, Letter 13, in *The Fathers of the Church Medieval Continuation: The Letters of Peter Damian, 1-30*, Trans., Owen J. Blum (Washington: Catholic University of America Press, 1989), 131.

[6] Ibid., 131.

that general disgust, he had competition for legitimacy. Pope Sylvester III, who had been kicked out of Rome by Benedict IX to start his second term, was still out there and still claiming that he was the legitimate pope and not Gregory. But even worse for Gregory was that Benedict himself had second thoughts about his own resignation. [7]

With three contenders for the papacy, and enough scandal to go around, the new Holy Roman Emperor Henry III decided to get involved. Prompted by his own personal confessor and a letter from the holy abbot of the Benedictine Monastery of Cluny, St. Odilo, Henry knew he had to intervene. [8] So, taking a large retinue of clerics and soldiers he crossed the alps in the fall of 1046 and by December he had called all the papal contenders to a meeting at the northern Italian town of Sutri. Gregory and Sylvester both showed up; Benedict did not. At the meeting of bishops, each was told to state their case. Gregory pleaded that he thought what he had done was okay at the time, even though now he realized it didn't look great. He wrote, "Before God I declare to you, my brethren, that, in acting as I did, I thought to win grace from God. But as I now perceive the craft of the Evil One, tell me what I must do." [9]

The answer was of course that Gregory had to resign for the good of the Church, and though he didn't want to, Gregory eventually acquiesced. [10] He resigned the papacy and went into exile in

---

[7] Mann 254.

[8] Ibid., 259.

[9] Ibid., 260.

[10] Though this is disputed in the sources, some suggest that the emperor simply deposed Gregory, others that he willingly resigned, albeit

Germany. Sylvester III and Benedict IX were both formally deposed by the council of Sutri, and then a new Pope was elected, a German who took the name Pope Clement II. Henry returned to Germany, hoping that the controversy was now settled and a truly reforming bishop was pope, but it was not to be. Clement II died within a year of being elected on October 9, 1047. The suddenness of his illness both provoked speculation that he was poisoned by the partisans of Benedict IX and prompted the Roman people to rise up against the German order imposed upon them.

While most historians rule out foul play in Clement's death, it was nevertheless perfect timing for Benedict. Henry was back in Germany and unable to interfere directly. His authority over the Roman population, who didn't like being ruled by a German emperor from far away, was weak at best. Benedict, aided by a generous amount of money which he spread around, was welcomed back to Rome on November 8, 1047, and was recognized as the pope, again. Thus, Pope Benedict IX began his third term on the Chair of Peter, and now we can account for the discrepancy in the numbering of the pontiffs. Pope Benedict's third and thankfully final term in Rome was short lived. By July 17, 1048, he had been deposed again by Emperor Henry III and a new Pope, Damasus II had been installed in Rome.

---

under pressure. See Antonio Sennis, "Gregorio VI, in *Enciclopedia dei Papi*, https://www.treccani.it/enciclopedia/gregorio-vi_%28Enciclopedia-dei-Papi%29/

Why does the Lord allow scandal?

There is a famous story found in the great Italian author Boccaccio's masterpiece *The Decameron* about scandal in Rome. The
story starts with two friends in Paris, a Catholic and a Jew, both of
whom were successful merchants and were recognized as upstand-
ing members of the community. The Catholic was constantly trying to convince his Jewish friend to convert to the faith, and little
by little his friend was convinced. However, before becoming
Catholic he made one condition; he would have to go to Rome
himself and see the Pope and the Roman curia to see how they
lived. His friend was distraught and tried to dissuade him from going, thinking to himself, "If he goes to the court of Rome and sees
the iniquitous and foul life which the clergy lead there, so far from
turning Christian, had he been converted already, he would without doubt relapse into Judaism."[11] Nevertheless, the Jewish merchant was determined to go. When he got to Rome, he discovered
things just as his Catholic friend had feared; the Pope and the clergy there were living horrible, scandalous lives in no way in accord
with the Gospel.

The Catholic merchant nervously awaited his friend's return,
and when they were able to meet up again the Jewish merchant
surprised his colleague by saying he was ready to become Catholic.
The Catholic was dumbfounded; didn't he see how horrible the
clergy in Rome were living their lives? His friend replied that in-

---

[11] Giovanni Boccaccio, *The Decameron*, Trans. J.M. Rigg,
https://www.gutenberg.org/cache/epub/3726/pg3726-images.html, I,2.

deed, it was horrible—it seemed like everyone in Rome was trying their hardest "to devise how best and most speedily they may bring the Christian religion to nought and banish it from the world."[12] However, he realized that while everyone in Rome, even the pope, were destroying the faith by their scandalous lives, the faith itself still grew and shined out in the world in truth and goodness. Therefore, he reasoned, it must have "the Holy Spirit for its foundation and support."[13]

When confronted with scandal in the Church, some version of this story is often told. Yes, there is scandal, but the Holy Spirit is still in charge. The problem with this approach is that besides seeming trite and dismissive of the real damage caused by scandalous behavior of members of the Church, it doesn't really grapple with the situation appropriately. Scandal can be incredibly harmful and lead to many people turning away from the truths of the faith and the channels of grace which are the sacraments. Indeed, our Lord, in addressing the evil of scandal, says, "It would be better for you if a millstone were hung around your neck and you were thrown into the sea than for you to cause one of these little ones to stumble" (Luke 17:2). Scandal can cause real psychological and spiritual damage, both in the initial evil act and in its later ramifications. Benedict IX's wild papacy was incredibly harmful to the Church and to the faithful—even those who were strongest in the faith hung their heads in shame when his name was mentioned.

---

[12] Boccaccio, I,2.
[13] Ibid.

Why does the Lord allow this to happen? The popes of the dark ages aside, there has been scandal throughout the history of the Church which has caused tremendous pain and turned many away from the faith. Our own time is replete with some of the most horrific acts of scandal of them all. Why? This question falls into the same category as some of the other big "why" questions that humanity has grappled with over the millennia. Why does God permit evil? Why do bad things happen to good people? Why does his providential care of the world allow the seemingly random natural events of immense suffering such as famines, floods, and pandemics?

It's difficult to answer such questions in a way that is simple and satisfying. That was not the approach that the Lord himself took. Jesus Christ enters our human suffering, our weakness, our meanness; he doesn't take it away magically. Like the master of the house in the parable, he does not immediately pull up the weeds of human misery and sin sewn by the enemy. He allows them to continue to grow alongside the wheat of the redeemed until the proper time, lest the wheat itself die (Matt 13:24-30). Even within the circle of his own chosen Apostles, he willingly admitted the one *he knew* would betray him. Judas was chosen, Judas was commissioned, Judas was ordained and communed in the first Eucharist, and Jesus knew all along the darkness in his heart.

Jesus's own ministry was the occasion of scandal, though not on the moral level. He was seen associating with tax collectors and sinners. He acted in contradistinction to the settled religious laws of the time. And his torture and death as a common criminal was utterly abhorrent to the sensibilities of the population of Palestine at the time. This was not how the Messiah would come; crucifixion was shameful. St. Paul speaks of this reality, writing, "For Jews demand signs and Greeks desire wisdom, but we proclaim Christ crucified, a stumbling block (*scandalon*; a scandal) to Jews and foolishness to Gentiles, but to those who are the called, both Jews and Greeks, Christ the power of God and the wisdom of God" (1 Cor 1:22-24). How many potential followers turned away from Jesus because they were scandalized by what he said and did? "When many of his disciples heard it, they said, 'This teaching is difficult; who can accept it?'" (John 6:60). And yet it was through the scandal of the cross, through his immersion into the fallen world of humanity, that Christ brought salvation to the world.

Loud cries and tears

In the Cathedral of Orvieto in central Italy there is a richly decorated chapel just off the main nave of the Church called the Chapel of the Madonna di San Brizio. Here, the Italian artist Luca Signorelli was commissioned to paint a series of frescos depicting the end of the world. One of the first frames appears to be a scene of Jesus preaching. Distracted by the pretty intense scenes of judgment and damnation on other panels, it is easy to set this early painting aside as a standard trope in religious artwork. Jesus stands on a pedestal and people stand around him from all over the world listening intently. However, something is off in the depiction. Taking a little more time, you can see a demon standing behind Jesus, speaking in his ear. Then you might notice that it looks like the demon is directing Jesus, controlling him. Finally, it hits you: this is clearly the resurrected Jesus, but he doesn't have any wounds. The hands pointing to his heart, the feet on the pedestal—there are no marks of the nails. It is not Jesus at all. It is the Antichrist.

Jesus's suffering and death was the heart of God's plan of salvation for the world. A *deus ex machina* where God simply took away evil was not good enough. He needed to enter into the suffering of the world. The author of the Letter to the Hebrews makes this very clear,

> In the days of his flesh, Jesus[a] offered up prayers and supplications, with loud cries and tears, to the one who was able to save him from death, and he was heard because of his reverent submission. Although he was a Son, he learned obedience through what he suffered; and having been made perfect, he became the source of eternal salvation for all who obey him, having been designated by God a high priest according to the order of Melchizedek. (Heb 5:7-10)

It was only by entering completely into the life of humanity and its alienation from God that Jesus could truly save us. Cardinal Albert Vanhoye writes commenting on this passage, "Christ has pushed to its limit his identification with mankind, he has descended to the depths of their destress, and... he has opened this same distress by his suppliant prayer and his agonized constancy, to the transforming action of God..."[14]

---

[14] Albert Vanhoye, *Old Testament Priests and the New Priest* (Gracewing, 2009), 137.

God does not save us without us, St Augustine writes. As we have already seen in an earlier chapter, God's salvation is not premised on conquest but on love, love that requires a free response. Jesus does not take away all suffering; he enters it and transforms it into a profound act of love. Love is greater than suffering and the true essence of our salvation. By taking the scandalous path of suffering, Jesus opens the door to real intimacy. "For we do not have a high priest who is unable to sympathize with our weaknesses, but we have one who in every respect has been tested as we are, yet without sin. Let us therefore approach the throne of grace with boldness, so that we may receive mercy and find grace to help in time of need" (Heb 4:15-16). By freely uniting our own sufferings with that of Christ, suffering is transformed into the most perfect act of love, and the burdens of our souls are lifted.

The Suffering of the Mystical Body

Though Jesus is no longer physically present on earth in his human body, his presence continues in his mystical body the Church. And just as Christ's physical body bore the marks of pain and suffering and the scandal of the Cross, Christ's mystical body bears the marks of human weakness and sinfulness. The Church is both holy and imperfect. It is holy because it is an extension of Christ who did not sin. It is imperfect because through the Church Christ reconciles sinners to the Father. As the Second Vatican Council writes, "Christ, 'holy, innocent and undefiled' (Heb. 7:26) knew nothing of sin (2 Cor. 5:21), but came only to expiate the sins of the people (cf. Heb 2:17). The Church, however, clasping sinners

to her bosom, at once holy and always in need of perfection, follows constantly the path of penance and renewal."[15]

The reality of human freedom and the need for mercy means
an imperfect Church in this life. If the way to salvation requires us
to freely enter a relationship with Christ through his Church, then
by necessity humans must have the ability to choose against Christ,
even members of the hierarchy. It is not only the really scandalous
and egregious sinners who contribute to this imperfection, as the
Catechism states, "All members of the Church, including her min-
isters, must acknowledge that they are sinners."[16] Every minor sin I
commit, even if done in secret, harms the Body of Christ. Yet
through the Church still we are purified and healed. Christ in his
mercy turns no one away, even the most heinous of sinners, and
his love pursues every lost sheep.

Pope Benedict IX was no exception; he, too, was pursued by the
mercy of God. Historians disagree on the details, but most accounts state that after several more failed attempts to regain the
papal throne, Benedict may have ended his life doing penance in
the monastery of Grottaferrata. It is said that the great St. Leo IX
prayed on his deathbed for Benedict's conversion, and the grace of
that saintly prelate's dying breaths may have been effective in mys-
teriously converting the ex-pope's heart.[17] The tradition of the
monastery was that Benedict gave up his pretensions to the papacy

---

[15] Second Vatican Council, *Lumen Gentium* in *Vatican Council II
Vol. 1: The Conciliar and Postconciliar Documents*, ed. Austin Flannery
(Northport: Costello Publishing Company, 1998), no. 8.

[16] *Catechism of the Catholic Church*, no. 827.

[17] Capitani, "Benedetto IX".

and, under the tutelage of the abbot St. Bartholomew, did penance for his sins and died a holy death.[18] Christ does not give up on anyone, even the most scandalous, and through the Church, in the mysteries of his plan, all are brought to salvation.

An Act of Faith

The fact that God allows the weeds to grow with the wheat is tough for the average Catholic to accept. The heinous nature of the scandal in the church very often drowns out in our hearts the truths of the nature of the Church and the reality of Grace. Our response to scandal should not be in any way to downplay or accept it, but rather to cling to Christ even more. When the disciples were scandalized by his teaching on the Eucharist, the Lord asked the Apostles, "Do you also wish to go away?" Peter's response with characteristic boldness, is a phrase which should be our prayer when scandalized: "Lord, to whom can we go? You have the words of eternal life. We have come to believe and know that you are the Holy One of God" (John 6:67-68). It is certainly not easy to cling to Christ in the darkness, but faith sustains us and enables us to peer through the murk of scandal and see the radiance of Christ shine in His mystical body.

---

[18] Mann, 293.

Chapter 7

Pope Gelasius II and Papal Poetry

How to Write with Papal Style

There are many reasons why men have been chosen to be Pope or to serve in the Papal bureaucracy. Pope Fabian was selected for his role because a bird landed on his head and those present who were trying to choose a new bishop of Rome recognized this unique circumstance as a sign from the Holy Spirit! Several popes moved up the ranks of the Roman Curia primarily because of their skill in chanting the Mass and the beauty of their voices. Many others, of course, are chosen because of their administrative ability or their personal holiness. John of Gaeta attracted the attention of the papacy because he was a great writer and scribe.

John of Gaeta was a Benedictine monk at the great Italian abbey of Monte Cassino during the 11th century. At that time, Monte Cassino was the heart of a great cultural awakening after the dark ages, under the direction of its holy abbot Desiderius, the future Pope Blessed Victor III. It was truly a golden age for the monastery, with over 200 monks working and praying in the abbey, and artists and craftsmen from all over the Mediterranean constructing the new basilica church. The library at the abbey flourished as well, and it was there that John of Gaeta was educated and cut his teeth copying books and preparing documents.

When his abbot was elected Pope Victor III, John of Gaeta came with him to help in his administration in Rome, and when Blessed Urban II succeeded Victor III, John was appointed papal chancellor. The reason for this appointment, his biographer tells us, is that John could and should bring a certain amount of beauty and eloquence to papal documents.[1] From ancient times, dating perhaps as far back as the papacy of St. Leo the Great, the correspondence of the Pope had been written in a particular poetic style called the *cursus leonitus*. This style was marked by a rhythmic stressing of certain syllables in Latin, so that all papal correspondence was written in what amounts to a poetic meter. During the dark ages, from around the 9th century until Blessed Urban II, it seems like that style had dropped out of papal communications.[2] As the papacy recovered its stature during the renewal of the church in the 11th and 12th centuries, there was a desire to restore the beauty and style of papal correspondence.

Enter John of Gaeta, who, having been well-trained in scholarly work as a monk at Monte Cassino, was tasked with improving the poetic quality of the Papal documents. Whether he completely re-introduced the *cursus* method of metrical writing as his biographer said, or whether he merely was tasked with improving its quality as scholars today suggest, it is clear that there was a lot of attention placed on making sure papal communications were beautiful.[3] In that same vein, John also oversaw the inclusion of miniscule, or

---

[1] Horace Mann, *Lives of the Popes...*, Vol. VIII, 123.

[2] Tore Janson, *Prose Rhythm in Medieval Latin*, 46.

[3] Jansen, 64.

lowercase letters, in papal documents.[4] In ancient Rome, scribal work was done primarily in capital letters, or majuscule scripts, but during the middle ages scribes began to work in miniscule, in order to improve the readability of texts and allow scribes to work efficiently. This practice had been underway for several centuries before it was finally adopted by Rome during John's tenure as Papal Chancellor. After serving faithfully, organizing the Papal chancery and bringing an enhanced eloquence to the popes' documents, John of Gaeta was elected Pope himself in 1118 and took the name Gelasius II.

"We cannot forget that beauty"

It may surprise us to find a Pope chosen ostensibly because of his scribal eloquence. Wouldn't management skills and pastoral ability be better prerequisites for the Chair of Peter? And while we can be pretty sure it wasn't just because of his promotion of poetry and lowercase letters that Gelasius II was elected pope, the importance given to this seemingly obscure aspect of the life of the Church seems out of place. Who really cares if Papal documents are written in poetry? Could you imagine if this were still the case today with encyclical letters needing to be set into meter or rhyme? You would be forgiven for thinking this is merely medieval pedantry and something we have thankfully left in the dust in our modern system of communication.

---

[4] Mann, 125.

And yet there is a lot to be learned from Gelasius II. The work he did in the Papal Chancery points to two broader themes that we would do well to ponder. The first is that beauty is important, indeed so important that it would even be worth investing energy and talent into promoting its spread. Beauty is defined rather ploddingly by St. Thomas as that which is pleasant to apprehend.[5] It is the product of a certain right ordering of things, either materially or spiritually, that is attractive. And while that all sounds incredibly dry and lacking the artistic verve that a true connoisseur of beauty would possess, it does strike at something deep and true. True beauty is related inextricably to goodness.

For a period, I was assigned to give tours of the great Basilica of St. Peter in Rome to English-speaking pilgrims. While we waited through the seemingly endless and ever-shifting lines to get through security, I would describe some of the history of the construction of the Church and the various features of the square and make small talk with the people on my tour. They would want to know about good places to get gelato and would tell me their anxieties about catching the right train to their next destination and what they were planning to do when they returned home. Amidst the unpleasant jostling of the crowds and the hot Roman sun, it was easy to focus on the mundane. However, once we entered the doors of the Basilica, everything changed. Jaws would drop, men and women would tear up, and all those mundane thoughts disappeared overwhelmed by the beauty of the space. There is a line in C.S. Lewis' *The Magician's Nephew* that describes perfectly the ex-

---

[5] St. Thomas Aquinas, *ST*, I-II, q. 27, a. 1.

perience these tourists-become-pilgrims had. When an old cockney cab driver hears the inexpressibly beautiful music of creation, he stops and exclaims, "I'd ha' been a better man all my life if I'd known there were things like this."[6]

St. John Paul II described beauty as "a key to the mystery and a call to transcendence. It is an invitation to savour life and to dream of the future." He continues, "It stirs that hidden nostalgia for God which a lover of beauty like Saint Augustine could express in incomparable terms: 'Late have I loved you, beauty so old and so new: late have I loved you!'."[7] This connection to transcendence is key to understanding the importance of beauty. Beauty breaks through our hard shells of routine and narrow mundane views of the world and forces us to think deeper thoughts, to contemplate more profound truths. It draws us out of ourselves and enables us to see a glimpse of the greater goodness and order of God's plan for creation.

Beauty is profoundly evangelical. A potential convert may spend years learning various truths of the faith and not truly be opened to God's grace. Then, in one instant, pierced by a beautiful painting or an eloquent verse or a euphonious harmony, her heart all of a sudden is open in ways it never was before. Vladimir, the king of Kievan Rus', sent servants to determine which religion he and his people should adopt; it was an experience of beauty which

---

[6] C.S. Lewis, "The Magician's Nephew" in *The Chronicles of Narnia* (New York: Harper Collins, 2001), 62.

[7] John Paul II, *Letter to Artists*, https://www.vatican.va/content/john - paul-ii/en/letters/1999/documents/hf_jp-ii_let_23041999_artists.html, 16.

convicted them. The emissaries were led into the great church of Hagia Sophia in what is now Istanbul and took part in the orthodox liturgy. They were transfixed, and on returning home they reported the following to their king,

> We knew not whether we were in heaven or on earth. For on earth there is no such splendor or such beauty, and we are at a loss how to describe it. We only know that God dwells there among men, and their service is fairer than the ceremonies of other nations. *For we cannot forget that beauty.*[8]

Beauty enables one to have an experience with the ineffable God, the God who is beyond comprehension, who transcends all our human categories, and yet deigns to show us his love. Beauty expresses something which cannot be expressed in words alone, and for that reason pierces the heart.

The Christian faith is a sacramental faith. A sacrament is, as every well catechized child can tell you, "an outward sign of an inward grace." God works interiorly, changing the soul through grace, and that interior action is manifested and enabled by a corresponding outward sign. The washing of the soul in baptism is made known through an outward washing of water. The love of Christ for his Church is made known through the outward sign of

---

[8] *The Russian Primary Chronicle*, trans. Samuel Hazard Cross & Olgerd P. Scherbowitz-Wetzor (Cambridge: The Medieval Academy of America, 1953), 111. (my emphasis)

the love of a husband and a bride. While it is enough that the right words and gestures be performed in order for the grace to flow, in order for a sacrament to be truly effective, the outward sign must reflect the beauty of the grace that is being given.[9] Something spectacular, neigh miraculous, happens when a Sacrament is received; its outward sign ought to reflect that interior reality.

This is why church buildings must be beautiful, why music must elevate the soul, and even why our warm welcome to the stranger or the suffering must be genuine. Our outward actions must reflect the beauty within. Which means that even obscure papal proclamations ought to be eloquent. The work of the Vatican is not merely the work of any old (indeed, very old, ancient!) bureaucracy. Every papal action, however insignificant, is caught up in the work of the Apostle Peter who was charged by Christ to "feed my sheep" (John 21:15). The purpose of the papacy is at its foundation pastoral, bringing the diverse flocks of Christ into good pasture so that they may be fed and flourish. This is a beautiful purpose! So, it stands to reason that the instruments of that end ought in themselves to reflect that beauty. Even on the level of the scribal or the typographical, beauty enhances and elucidates the truth, and ugliness conversely can mar it.[10] Beauty is not optional, merely something nice to have alongside one's faith; it is essential.

---

[9] See for example St. Thomas Aquinas' understanding of devotion and beauty in the sacramental order.

[10] See for example the introductory essay in Robert Bringhurst, *The Elements of Typographic Style,* Point Roberts: Hartley & Marks Publishers, 2004)

The Means Matter

Scribal work was hard and took time. A good scribe was able to produce beautifully crafted words which were readable and made the words speak even more eloquently. Even today, when one opens a word document to write out a text, the choice of typesetting and font, the attention to the details of letter spacing and kerning (the spacing of letters in sentences) make a difference in the message the text intends to communicate. As the typographer Robert Bringhurst writes, "Well-chosen words deserve well-chosen letters; these in their turn deserve to be set with affection, intelligence, knowledge and skill."[11] A medieval scribe was a specially-trained craftsman, who spent years practicing his art and produced brilliant manuscripts which today are valued as works of art. The papal scribes in the chancery of John of Gaeta paid attention to the details of every poetic ending and miniscule letter.

The time and attention taken in making sure basic papal documents were metrically eloquent and well-written certainly must have added to the scribal load of John of Gaeta and his coworkers. The modern mind, which is wont to rush off a thought in a text message or a tweet, might find the work of the medieval Vatican scribe arcane and inefficient. Who cares how the message is presented so long as the message gets through? But this attention to detail reveals another truth, *how* we do something and not just *why* we do something matters a great deal. This is a well-known truth in moral theology, one that has become commonplace and proverbial,

---

[11] Bringhurst, 18.

"the ends don't justify the means." In order for an action to be a good one, it is not enough that your intention be good, *the way* you bring about that end must also be good. My good intention of building the greatest Lego sculpture ever and the evangelical beauty that would result, do not justify the *means* I employ to bring it about, namely my theft of millions of toy bricks. How I do something matters in determining the moral quality of an action.

While on the surface you would think most people would not disagree with this fundamental truth, there is a common temptation for all humans to rush to the ends and neglect the means. Impatience drives us to skip through the necessary steps and cut to the chase; we want the results without the work. This was often the desire for me while doing chores as a child. I could do things the right way, which took time and effort, or I could take the short cut and be done sooner. In the short term, I completed my task quicker, but those short cuts would need to be repaid eventually.

The temptation to sacrifice the means for the sake of the end is present throughout our society. We see this in the political realm where politicians and voters of every stripe would rather reject the process of democracy in favor of their own politically desirable results. The temptation is present in our moral lives when we tell white lies to maintain a relationship rather than do the harder work of confronting difficult truths. Even the works of some Catholic artists and authors betray this temptation. The more mediocre author merely ties up stories in a nice Catholic bow, driving home a Catholic message but without paying attention to the more difficult work of character development and the beauty of prose. The

values of the faith are articulated, but at the cost of beauty and eloquence. The means matter; how we do something is important!

Setting aside the means in order to expediently reach the end is
in most cases folly. We might reach our goal, but that goal will be
bereft of the goodness which made us pursue it in the first place.
This is particularly true in our spiritual lives. Often, we think about
getting to heaven in terms of a checklist. St. Peter will wait at the
pearly gates, and we need to be able to demonstrate that yes, we fed
the poor, yes, we went to mass, yes, we were good people. Being a
Christian in that mindset would seem to consist in completing several outward tasks, and we might be tempted to take shortcuts to
accomplish them. Rather than embark on the more difficult journey of conversion of heart, we try to buy off God by going to
church and doing good deeds. As Pope John Paul II writes, "Following Christ is not an outward imitation, since it touches man at
the very depths of his being. Being a follower of Christ means becoming conformed to him who became a servant even to giving
himself on the Cross (cf. Phil 2:5-8)."[12] Going to heaven doesn't
permit shortcuts because God can't be bought off with cheap bribes
of quick prayers and alms; he knows that the only thing which will
satisfy us is the transformation of our hearts.

We inherently recognize the importance of the means when we
tell stories about people who failed to reach their goal but would
rather stay true to their principles than succeed. The stories of the
martyrs immediately spring to mind, from the brothers put to

---

[12] John Paul II, *Veritatis Splendor*, https://www.vatican.va/content/
john-paul-ii/en/encyclicals/documents/hf_jp-ii_enc_06081993_veritatis-
splendor.html, 21.

death in Maccabees to our modern-day confessors. They chose to die rather than to use an evil means to survive, even when that means was as simple as putting a single grain of incense on the altar of the pagan gods. But we also see the same story in literature and popular culture. Countless novels tell the story of the man who fights the hopeless fight, not hoping to succeed but simply to do good. Other stories show what happens when you sacrifice principle in the name of the ends. In films like *The Man who Shot Liberty Valance* and *The Dark Knight Rises,* characters lie in order to expediently bring about a certain good, and at first it seems like everyone is happy. But the lie festers, and in the end leads to greater conflict and a deeper darkness. Even if it means the seeming triumph of evil, as when the martyr is killed, it is better to choose to act well than to sacrifice principle for the sake of the end—to pay attention to doing the right thing and doing it well.

We are seemingly a long way from the medieval scribe trying to produce beautiful and poetic ecclesial documents, but the principles that unite the martyr and the papal chancellor are the same. John of Gaeta's seemingly pedantic devotion to beautiful writing, even in the most obscure of circumstances, reveals the inherent goodness of doing things the right way. The means of any action are not mere external realities, however. In the end, beautiful typography will not get you to heaven, just as wearing pants is not detrimental to the healthy spiritual life. His attention to the minutia of meter was not the hoop God demanded for him to jump through to attain salvation. Rather, it demonstrated the love and care with which he approached a seemingly mundane task. The result was a beauty which was eloquent. Each individual document might not rank in importance in the western literary canon, but the overall accomplishment of bedecking the papal correspondence with poetry added to the evangelical beauty of the mission of the successor of St. Peter. Although now largely forgotten by the faithful, through his steadfast attention to detail, Gelasius II continued to build on the rock of Peter the beautiful edifice of the Church.

Chapter 8

Pope Liberius does not Goof off

Reverence for the Word at a Young Age

If you have heard of Pope Liberius at all, it's usually in a fairly negative context. As you scan through the list or perhaps a poster of all the popes, he stands out for the simple reason that he doesn't have a "saint" in front of his name. Every pope before him, from St. Peter on down, is listed as a saint; Liberius is the first pope who isn't. The reason for this is caught up in controversies surrounding the heresy of Arianism in the middle of the fourth century. There are various opinions on Pope Liberius' conduct and whether he deserves the infamy he has received. Some say he caved to political pressure and violence and embraced the Arian heresy in order to save his life. Others, including the Eastern Orthodox Church that recognizes him as a saint, assert his firmness in the truth at a time when every other bishop was caving to the Arians. Regardless of the results of this debate, there is another area of his life worth bringing to light, and that is his childhood.

It's rare that we know anything about the early lives of the more ancient popes. Pope Liberius is a great exception. Inscribed on the fourth century pope's tomb is a long Latin poem which, beginning with his childhood, winds its way through the pontiff's life. The section describing his childhood reads as follows:

As a youth, when you began to speak sweet words,

You were made by talent a holy reader of the scriptures

As soon as your tongue sounded the law more than words,

Beloved by God was your aforementioned simple childhood,

With no wicked trickery, the page being embellished,

In the art of reading during such a just and pure service.

You were also simple in mind as a youth,

Mature in soul at a burning age, modest

Distant, prudent, meek, grave, sound, just;

This was a golden life for you as a benign lector.[1]

To better understand what is being described, we need to take ourselves back to ancient Christian Rome. As has been the case throughout history, at that time boys often served in various capacities in Christian liturgies. Today, children serve as altar servers and lectors, and it was the same back then. The young Pope Liberius served in his formative years as a lector, reading the various psalms and scriptural readings in the great basilicas of Rome from an early age. He was probably a part of a school of young readers which not only organized and scheduled each reader, but trained and educated them.[2] So, like Catholic school children of today, the

---

[1] Orazio Marucchi, *Christian Epigraphy; An Elementary Treatise with a Collection of Ancient Christian Inscriptions Mainly of Roman Origin* (Cambridge: Cambridge University Press, 1912), 415-416. Translation from Latin by Rev. Joseph Rampino.

[2] L. Duchesne, *Christian Worship: Its Origin and Evolution.* Trans M.L. McClure (London: Society for Promoting Christian Knowledge, 1904), 348.

young Liberius regularly served as a reader at Mass along with his classmates and friends.

Also, like today, young boys of ancient Rome often lacked virtue and maturity, even, God forbid, in the august and sacred spaces that dotted the city. Nearly everyone who has served at Mass has had some experience of goofing off during the liturgy, trying to get your friends to laugh, jabbing your grade school nemeses in the neck with the paten at communion, or mocking the priest behind his back. It's a common part of growing up and has been for centuries. Liberius' epitaph assumes that often the young readers of the Roman basilicas purposely messed up in order to make their friends laugh, embellishing the page with "wicked trickery".

It seems that Liberius' conduct as a young man bucked the trend. His solemnity and maturity in reading the scripture in the liturgy was so remarkable that it earned a spot in the inscription on his tomb. Along with many other youthful virtues, Liberius took the liturgy seriously and approached it with reverence beyond his years. As his epitaph says, "Mature in soul at a burning age, modest, distant, prudent, meek, grave, sound, just."[3]

Reverence v. Joy?

There is another way of looking at this epitaph. Instead of seeing youthful maturity one could look at the young Liberius as an adolescent stick-in-the-mud, unable to take things lightly. There

---

[3] Orazio Marucchi, *Christian Epigraphy*, Trans. J. Armine Willis (Cambridge: University Press, 1912), 415-416.

seems to be a spectrum in the modern mind regarding the liturgy with solemn reverence on one side and lighthearted joy on the other. With this way of looking at things, those who trend towards the former end up as pharisaical curmudgeons while those who trend towards the latter are seen as flaky free spirits. Most Christians can recognize characters from their own parish on either side of this dichotomy, and both sides probably have something to say for themselves. But is this really how we should view the relationship between reverence and joy?

In Act II of Shakespeare's *Much Ado about Nothing*, Count Claudio is asked why he is so silent after his engagement to his beloved. He responds, "Silence is the perfectest herald of joy: I were but little happy, if I could say how much."[4] His reply shows that there is depth to joy which is greater than mere giddiness—that there is a type of joy which is so deep that lighthearted banter or capricious joking, or even description itself, is unworthy. Claudio could have described his happiness if it were more superficial, but the joy of giving his heart to his beloved is a mystery too great for words, and only silence can herald it.

This type of joy does not exclude reverence; indeed, true reverence feeds it. St. Thomas Aquinas writes that devotion in the exercise of worship causes as a "direct and principal effect" the "spiritual joy of the mind."[5] He explains that devotion is caused in two ways when we go to Mass. First, it's sparked by a consideration of God's goodness: we see in the liturgy God pouring out his whole

---

[4] Shakespeare, *Much Ado about Nothing*, Act II Scene I.
[5] St. Thomas Aquinas, *ST* II-II, Q. 82, a. 4

self to us through the sacrifice of Christ on the cross. Confronted with this radical and extravagant act of selfless love, we cannot but experience profound and lasting joy and in turn desire to serve him more fervently. Likewise, we see also in the liturgy how we have failed and turned away from God. We see our hearts' infidelity more clearly by the light of his goodness. This prompts a certain sorrow at our weakness, but at the same time joy in recognizing that even in our failings we are loved magnificently.[6]

C.S. Lewis writes about this spiritual joy in *The Last Battle*, stating, "He knew why they were laughing and joined in the laugh himself. But very quickly they all became grave again: for, as you know, there is a kind of happiness and wonder that makes you serious. It is too good to waste on jokes."[7] The context of joy and the source of that joy matters. The greatness of the expression of Jesus's love on the Cross, which is the heart of the liturgy, is a font of great joy, but a joy which isn't foolish. Pope Liberius's devotion to the word of God was not necessarily dry and matter of fact; it could have been the wellspring of deep and meaningful spiritual joy.

At the same time, for reverence to be more than pedantic adherence to rubrics and traditions, it has to be alive with spiritual joy. The purpose of solemnity in the liturgy is to engage the soul in contemplation of these deeper realities of the faith.[8] Excessively stoic behavior in the liturgy is not healthy. At some point, the joy of what is being celebrated has to take root; otherwise, it's just hyp-

---

[6] Ibid.

[7] C.S. Lewis, "The Last Battle", in *The Chronicles of Narnia* (New York: Harper Collins, 2001), 764.

[8] St. Thomas Aquinas, *ST* II-II, Q. 82, a. 3.

ocritical playacting. This is the hypocrisy for which Jesus condemns the Pharisees, "Woe to you, scribes and Pharisees, hypo-
crites! For you are like whitewashed tombs, which on the outside
look beautiful, but inside they are full of the bones of the dead and
of all kinds of filth. So you also on the outside look righteous to
others, but inside you are full of hypocrisy and lawlessness" (Matt
23:27-28). Joy is the fruit that shows that the liturgy is working,
that we as participants really are encountering the tremendous love
of Christ. If it remains dry ritualism without that fruit, something
is not working. As one American Cardinal has said, "If you don't
enjoy doing Church, you are doing it wrong."

Why is Reverence Important?

Why this emphasis on reverence in the liturgy? Why was it so
important to note about young Pope Liberius that it made it onto
his epitaph? Reverence and devotion enable a deeper reception of
grace. While the sacraments infallibly communicate grace, provided we have the right intention, our disposition when receiving
them can change the quality of the grace we receive. Imagine three
items set on a table, a rock, a piece of wood, and a sponge. Someone pours exactly one cup of water on each, and what happens?
The same amount of water is given to each, but the rock soaks up
very little, the wood a little more, and the sponge a lot. Devotion,
according to St. Thomas, is the disposition of the soul which enables a more fruitful reception of grace.[9] It makes our hearts more

---

[9] St. Thomas Aquinas, *ST* III, q. 69, a. 8.

spongy, soaking up the abundant graces that are being poured out at every celebration of the sacraments.

Devotion, according to St. Thomas, is not just a feeling. You don't have to feel like you really believe, or really are in love, or are really in tune with God at Mass in order to be devout. In fact, devotion is the fruit of contemplation. It is a disposition of the soul to serve God with fervor and zeal prompted by a consideration of how good his love is and how little we deserve it. That fervor need not be a feeling; indeed, devotion is proven more when we *don't* feel fervor than when we do. By recognizing how much God loves us and how often we turn away from that love, our minds and our hearts are moved to respond, and we little by little are disposed to habitually and promptly return to him in worship. With that disposition we receive more fruitfully the graces given to us in the sacraments and our hearts are transformed with greater speed.

Devotion has an objective quality to it. It is not enough for the external aspects of the liturgy like the music or the architecture to evoke positive emotions; they need to call to mind the objective reality of God himself. St. Thomas Aquinas discusses this in particular when it comes to Church music. He says there is a distinction between music played for pleasure and music which evokes devotion.[10] It's not enough for the music in Church to be pleasurable; it has to lead us objectively towards the contemplation of God. Nostalgia and fashion can't be the shapers of the liturgy; rather, the reality of God himself and the mystery of his inner life and incarnation in Jesus are what guide how the Mass is celebrated.

---

[10] Ibid., II-II, q. 91, a. 2.

Hence the importance of reverence at Mass. As human beings, we need tangible reminders of God's loving kindness, of his majesty and power, of his mercy and forgiveness. St. Thomas writes that all the various signs and ceremonies, the splendor and the beauty of the liturgy is present primarily to spark devotion.[11] Think back to a time you were at Mass and the altar servers were not paying attention. Perhaps they forgot to bring something over to the altar or had the book on the wrong page, or maybe they were just joking with each other during an important part of the Mass. It immediately catches your attention and draws you out of the moment. You aren't thinking about Jesus so much as you are thinking about something going wrong. When everyone in the liturgy is doing what they are meant to be doing, you don't think about the individual, you just see the beauty and are able to think more about Jesus. When the readings are read beautifully, you don't think about the reader but about the message—when they are read poorly you think about the reader.

Reverence and attention to detail in the liturgy draw us into the mystery; they enable us to encounter Christ, to attend to his words and to the sacrament, and to prepare our hearts. While his epitaph acknowledges the young Pope Liberius' reverence, the people in the congregation wouldn't have been focusing on the reader so much as the word. His diligence enabled their devotion; his care helped them meet Jesus. Devotion and reverence need not be the domain of stuffiness! By reverently serving, we and those we en-

---

[11] See for example, St. Thomas Aquinas, *ST* II-II q. 82, a. 3, ad. 2.

counter are enabled to receive a greater and deeper joy. We encounter Christ, and his joy is in us and is complete (cf. John 15:11).

Chapter 9

Two Miracles and the Feast of Corpus Christi

A Pope in the Right Places at the Right Times

In the early part of the 13th century, a young girl named Juliana entered a convent in the city of Liege, in what is today Belgium. Juliana had a deep love of God and a burning passion to adore him at Mass and in the Blessed Sacrament. She would be so wrapped in prayer that her sisters at the convent were particularly worried that she would ruin her health by too much devotion. When Sr. Juliana was around sixteen years old, she had a vision in prayer. She saw a full moon, except there was one stripe of darkness crossing its face from end to end. The vision was brief, but it would recur several times over the course of her life.[1]

Confused and concerned as to what the vision could mean, Sr. Juliana turned to her superior in the convent, who had been her teacher from an early age. The sister told her that in general when it comes to visions to not be too caught up in them but to entrust them to God. It could be nothing; it could have just been a dream.[2] She consulted as well with local priests and religious to see if they could help her understand her vision, and they responded with similar answers. They suggested she put the vision out of her mind

---

[1] George Ambrose Bradbury, *The Life of St. Juliana of Cornillon* (London: Thomas Richardson and Sons, 1873), 33.

[2] Ibid., 34.

and humbly focus on Christ alone. The challenge was that the vision kept coming back. Sr. Juliana continually begged God that he stop giving her this grace, but it was to no avail.

Finally, after a long time of struggle, Sr. Juliana was given an answer. A voice during one of the visions explained to her what it meant. The moon had a dark spot on it because something was lacking in the Church. The voice said to her "that its lustrous brightness represented the different solemnities celebrated in the Church during the course of the year. The dark spot which obscured a part of the moon's lustre, signified the want of a certain feast, which it was God's will should be instituted; that this feast was to honour the most august and most holy Sacrament of the Altar..."[3] God wanted a new feast in the Church, a feast devoted to the Blessed Sacrament, and revealed it to Sr. Juliana to try and make it happen.

At first, following the advice of those she initially consulted, Sr. Juliana kept everything private out of a sense of humility. But eventually after twenty years or so without speaking about the vision she finally told some of her closer friends. They were moved, and formed what Pope Benedict XVI called, "a sort of "spiritual alliance" for the purpose of glorifying the Most Holy Sacrament."[4] They then consulted some of the more learned clerics in Liege to see what they thought about the vision. The task was given to a Fr. John of Lausanne, who then talked with some of his colleagues, including the Archdeacon James of Troyes and eventually the Bishop

---

[3] Ibid., 39

[4] Pope Benedict XVI, "General Audience 17 November 2010," https://www.ewtn.com/catholicism/library/st-juliana-of-cornillon-6285

Robert Torote.[5] The vision and the desire for a new feast dedicated to the Blessed Sacrament were embraced enthusiastically and the diocese of Liege set up locally the new feast, the celebration of *Corpus Christi*.

Not long after, in 1263 in the city of Bolsena in central Italy, a priest was celebrating Mass. He was a German priest, Fr. Peter, from the city of Prague, and he was on a pilgrimage to visit the holy sites in Rome.[6] While celebrating Mass, Fr. Peter struggled with a feeling which had plagued a lot of his priesthood. It was a feeling of doubt as to whether Jesus was really present in the Eucharist or whether it was just a pious symbol. He wanted to believe but struggled frequently with doubt when celebrating Mass, and this day was no exception.

Suddenly, as soon as he said the words of the Lord, "This is my body," blood started flowing out of the host, onto his hands, and down onto the clothes on the altar.[7] Fr. Peter was startled and confused—what was happening? The blood started to stain the corporal, the small white cloth on which the host is placed during Mass, and soaked through to the altar beneath. He stopped the celebration of Mass, gathered together the host and the cloth and returned to the sacristy. He then asked that he be taken to the next town over, the hill town of Orvieto, where Pope Urban IV was currently in residence. The Pope immediately took interest in the mir-

---

[5] Ivana Ait, "Urbano IV" in *Enciclopedia dei Papi,* https://treccani.it /enciclopedia/urbano-vi_%28Enciclopedia-dei-Papi%29/

[6] Joan Carrol Cruz, *Eucharistic Miracles* (Charlotte, TAN Publishing, 1987).

[7] Ibid.

acle and asked the bishop to bring the host and the cloth to Orvieto.

The connection between these two miracles was one person, the Archdeacon James of Troyes. He served as Archdeacon of Liege and knew St. Juliana personally. He was later elected Pope Urban IV and was present in Orvieto during the Eucharistic miracle at Bolsena. He had been in Liege when the bishop implemented the feast of Corpus Christi there, and now he was in a position to do even more. Inspired by the new miracle in Orvieto and remembering St. Juliana's vision, Pope Urban IV extended the feast of Corpus Christi to the whole Church. In the Papal Bull that established the feast, he wrote,

> Moreover we know that, while we were constituted in a lesser office, it was divinely revealed to certain Catholics that a feast of this kind should be celebrated generally throughout the Church. Therefore, to strengthen and exalt the Catholic Faith, we decree that, besides the daily memory that the Church makes of this Sacrament, there be celebrated a more solemn and special annual memorial. Then let the hearts and mouths of all break forth in hymns of saving joy; then let faith sing, hope dance, charity exult, devotion applaud, the choir be jubilant, and purity delight. Then let each one with willing spirit and prompt will come together, laudably fulfilling his duties, celebrating the Solemnity of so great a Feast.[8]

---

[8] Urban IV, *Transiturus*.

Pope Urban IV was in the right places at the right times, and inspired by two miraculous events, he formally established the feast of Corpus Christi, which we still celebrate today.

The History of Devotion to the Blessed Sacrament

It might seem strange to us that the Feast of Corpus Christi came so late in Church history. Wasn't there devotion to the Blessed Sacrament in the early Church? Why did it take almost thirteen centuries for this feast to be added? The establishment of the Feast of Corpus Christi by Pope Urban IV is the culmination of a longer process of the Church's growing in understanding and devotion to the Lord's real presence in the Eucharist. This growth flowed from early medieval theological controversies about how exactly Jesus makes himself present under the appearances of bread and wine. As the Church grappled with these intricate and important theological questions, she began to understand just how great a gift the Eucharist is.

Christians have always had a devotion to the Eucharist and an understanding that the Eucharist was Christ's true body and blood. We see in the writings of the earliest Church Fathers, some writing just decades after the resurrection of the Lord, a clear belief in the miracle which is the Blessed Sacrament. St. Ignatius of Antioch, writing around 110 AD, condemns those heretics who, "abstain from the Eucharist and from prayer, because they confess not the Eucharist to be the flesh of our Saviour Jesus Christ, which suffered for our sins, and which the Father, of His goodness, raised up again."[9] Likewise, St. Justin Martyr, another second century apologist, describes the Eucharist as,

> For not as common bread and common drink do we receive these; but in like manner as Jesus Christ our Saviour, having been made flesh by the Word of God, had both flesh and blood for our salvation, so likewise have we been taught that the food which is blessed by the prayer of His word, and from which our blood and flesh by transmutation are nourished, is the flesh and blood of that Jesus who was made flesh.[10]

The early Church knew and loved the Sacrament of the Lord's Body and Blood, from the very beginning of the Church's existence.

As the Church grew and matured, theologians started trying to understand how exactly Christ became present in the Blessed Sacrament. Like most theological controversies in the history of the Church, a theologian would posit a theory and the Church would react, saying it was out of bounds or not nuanced enough or didn't coincide with the Church's broader understanding. The most famous early medieval controversy about the Eucharist was initiated by the theologian Berengar of Tours in the eleventh century. Berengar promoted a more metaphorical understanding of Jesus's pre-

---

[9] St. Ignatius of Antioch, *Letter to the Smyrnaeans,* https://newadvent.org/fathers/0109.htm, ch. 7.

[10] Justin Martyr, *First Apology,* https://newadvent.org/fathers/0126.htm, Cap 66.

sence in the Eucharist: it was more a symbol than a reality. During Mass, the substance of the bread and wine remain just that, bread and wine. Symbolically, however they are changed in the minds of the faithful into a participation in the body and blood of Jesus.

In response to Berengar's teaching about the Eucharist, the Church articulated more fully the consistent teaching about the real presence of Jesus in the Blessed Sacrament. A series of meetings of theologians and prelates culminated in the Easter Synod of Pope Nicholas in 1059. At that gathering of churchmen, the Pope reaffirmed the teaching of the real presence of Jesus in the Eucharist and ordered greater liturgical signs of reverence for the reserved Blessed Sacrament in the tabernacle. It is from this Easter Synod that the practice of genuflecting before the tabernacle was mandated, something that every Catholic has ingrained in them from an early age. From then on, the theologians of the Church debated and considered what exactly the real presence meant, culminating in St. Thomas Aquinas's great work in the *Summa Theologica* and the establishment of the Feast of *Corpus Christi*.

The Development of Doctrine

It might seem disconcerting to the average Catholics that such pious rituals as genuflection are not as ancient as might be supposed. There is an anachronistic strain in us which wants every detail of our life of faith to be present at the Last Supper. We want Jesus to teach the Apostles how to celebrate adoration of the Blessed Sacrament and the Rite of Eucharistic Benediction or the proper color vestments for the priest to wear when hearing confessions. Otherwise, don't we give in to the cynics and the critics of the Church who say that all you believe is really just a pious accretion? That the Catholic faith is more medieval than biblical? Jesus never said anything about anointing with Chrism in the Bible or how to hold your hands or how to put out your tongue to receive communion. Doesn't that reality delegitimize the Catholic faith and practice?

Into this confusion comes the Church's understanding of the *development* of doctrine. Jesus did not spell out every aspect of the faith as taught in the catechism from the beginning; it developed over time. When we hear that, we can think that development means that the Cardinals and Pope in Rome thought up some new ideas of what to believe and said, "Let's give these a try." To the contrary, development of doctrine doesn't mean developing new truths of the faith so much as unpacking and understanding with greater depth the truths we were given by the Lord.

The images theologians turn to in order to understand how doctrines develop are usually drawn from the growth of plants. A seed planted in the ground does not become something else. The same DNA, and the same nature, is present in the seed as in the mature plant. You don't plant an avocado and see a pine tree grow up in its place. Everything that is needed for growth is already there. The grown plant is more itself, not something different altogether. So, too, the doctrines of the Church. Everything we believe about the Eucharist was already present when Jesus said to his apostles, "This is my body." But over the centuries the Church has unpacked what that means.

Doctrine can't develop contrary to the truths already taught by Christ two thousand years ago. As St. Vincent of Lerins axiomatically wrote in the fifth century, "Moreover, in the Catholic Church itself, all possible care must be taken, that we hold that faith which has been believed everywhere, always, by all."[11] There is one faith, one truth taught and believed in the Church, that given by Jesus Christ. But as St. Vincent continues, there is room for development,

[O]n condition that it be real progress, not alteration of the faith. For progress requires that the subject be enlarged in itself, alteration, that it be transformed into something else. The intelligence, then, the knowledge, the wisdom, as well of individuals as of all, as well of one man as of the whole Church, ought, in the course of ages and centuries, to increase and make much and vigorous progress; but yet only in its own kind; that is to say, in the same doctrine, in the same sense, and in the same meaning.[12]

As theologians and the faithful digest the truths taught by Christ and apply their minds and hearts to the contemplation of them, the truth can develop. It doesn't change the truth; there is never a moment when something Jesus taught was wrong is now right, but it does deepen our appreciation of it.

---

[11] St. Vincent of Lerins, *Commonitory*, https://www.newadvent.org/fathers/3506.htm, cap 6.

[12] Ibid., 54.

This is what happened with the Eucharist. From the earliest centuries of the Church, we have believed in the real presence of Christ in the Eucharist. But as philosophers, theologians, and mystics contemplated the gift more, they understood better just how beautiful of a gift it really is. This sparked greater devotion in the hearts of the faithful and prompted saints and popes to celebrate it with greater festivity and reverence. Added to that process was, of course, the providential role of Pope Urban IV, who happened to be in just the right places at the right times to experience two of God's Eucharistic miracles. The development of doctrine doesn't happen solely by way of the minds of humans; God's grace germinates the truths he planted.

A Poetic Epilogue

The story of the Feast of Corpus Christi would not be complete without one final famous anecdote. After Pope Urban IV instituted the solemnity in the liturgical calendar of the Church, he needed some poetic help writing the hymns and prayers that would be used when celebrating the feast. He turned to two of his close theological collaborators, St Thomas Aquinas and his Franciscan counterpart, St. Bonaventure. According to the story, one disputed by historians, St. Thomas presented the Pope with his work first, and upon hearing it Bonaventure destroyed his copies because of the beauty of his confrere's composition.[13] The Pope himself was in

---

[13] It is generally held by historians, due to the testimony of two of St. Thomas's students, that he was the author of the Office of Corpus Chris-

tears while he listened to the great theologian read his poetry. These poems might be the most well known of St. Thomas's works to Catholics today, verses of the great hymn *Pange Lingua* are sung every Holy Thursday and at the conclusion of Eucharistic Adoration. Not only then did the Eucharistic miracles experienced by Pope Urban provide the Church with a great feast, but also with some of her most enduring and beautiful poetry. Truly the work of providence!

---

ti, but the story with St. Bonaventure is from a later date. Cf James A. Weisheipl, *Thomas D'Aquino* (Garden City: Doubleday & Company, 1974), 177.

Chapter 10

St. Pius X and the Two Rings

In November of 1884, Giuseppe Sarto, a priest from a humble northern Italian family, was ordained the Bishop of Mantua. Returning home to his mother after his ordination to the episcopacy, the new bishop ran to his mother and hugged her like a little boy. Sarto's mother Margherita had spent most of her life doing peasant labor to help support her growing family, and now her son was a bishop. The new bishop Giuseppe proudly showed his mother his new episcopal ring, the symbol of the bishop's fidelity and devotion to his diocese. His mother, however, was not impressed. She turned to her son and pointing to her own wedding ring said, "Yes, Giuseppe, your ring is beautiful; but you would not have had it had I not had this."[1]

In 1903, Giuseppe Sarto traded his beautiful bishop's ring for a new one, the ring of the fisherman. He was elected Pope Pius X and during his coronation was given the traditional papal ring, a simple round ring with the pope's regnal name written in Latin and an image of St. Peter fishing engraved upon it. For several centuries the Popes used the fisherman's ring as their means of signing and sealing documents, and when a pope dies or resigns, the ring is ceremonially broken, showing that his authority to sign documents

---

[1] Igino Giordani, *Pius X: A Country Priest* (Milwaukee, Bruce Publishing Co., 1952), 37.

is no longer valid. It was this new ring, and the new responsibilities it symbolized, that Giuseppe Sarto would have to bear.

Sarto, like many who are eventually elected, did not want to be Pope. There is a story that before the conclave that elected him, he joked that he would either become the Pope or die. Every assignment he had up to that point had lasted exactly 9 years: assistant priest, pastor, chancellor of the diocese, bishop of Mantua, and Cardinal Archbishop of Venice. Every assignment had been for nine years, and on heading to the conclave he told a friend, that in order for that cycle to continue, he would either have to be elected Pope or die. His friend responded that he hoped it would be the former. The future pope replied, "And I for the latter, rather dead than pope."[2] When the balloting began and it became clear that the Cardinals were going to elect Sarto pope, he openly wept in front of them and begged them not to elect him.[3] This prompted the Cardinals to vote for him all the more. The American Cardinal Gibbons wrote after the fact, "It was that very adjuration, his grief, his profound humility and wisdom, that made us think of him all the more; we learnt to know him from his words as we could never have known him by hearsay."[4] When the deciding vote happened and the Cardinals asked him if he would accept he responded, "Would that this chalice might be far from me! Yet may the will of God be done!" He continued, "I accept it as a cross!"[5] Margherita

---

[2] Ibid.

[3] Giordani, 64.

[4] F.A. Forbes, Life of St. Pius X (New York, P.F. Kennedy, 1918), 66.

[5] Giordani, 67.

Sarto's son, the product of her simple wedding ring, was now the Pope.

Marriage and the Priestly Vocation

The insight that Pope Pius X's mother had about the relationship between their two rings touches on a beautiful and little understood truth: the vocations of marriage and the celibate priesthood reinforce one another. Often, we think it's the opposite. Either we think that marriage is for those who cannot embrace the lofty and spiritually superior vocation of celibacy and religious life, or we believe that celibates are those who either couldn't get married or don't like marriage. The two seem opposed or separate, not as intimately linked at St. Pius X's mother's quip suggests.

The first time I really understood the beauty of the celibate priesthood, I was visiting a wonderful Catholic family. They were parishioners at one of my summer assignments as a seminarian and invited me over to their house for an afternoon. I was struck by the beauty and goodness of the whole family; they were devoted to Christ, to each other, and were particularly happy. As I left their house, I thought to myself, "This is so good, I want this!" It was a thought which at first seemed to go contrary to the vocation I was discerning and would have been upsetting had the next thought that popped into my mind not reassured me. I realized in that moment that this was the gift I was going to give to God as a celibate priest, and it was such a good gift.

Celibacy is not a mere discipline; it is not avoiding a negative situation. It's not as if marriage is inherently imperfect and should be avoided. Rather, marriage is a good, a great good, and celibacy is the giving of that great good as a gift back to God. Only by knowing the true value and goodness of marriage, of seeing it as something to be desired and cherished, can celibacy be truly valued. Celibacy for the sake of the kingdom is not then a discipline that one has to do in order to be ordained; it is itself an act of supreme love to be sought for its own sake. As the Second Vatican Council writes, "And so the free choice of sacred celibacy has always been considered by the Church "as a symbol of, and stimulus to, charity": (42) it signifies a love without reservations; it stimulates to a charity which is open to all."[6] St. Pius X's ring was like his mother's a marriage ring, signifying his total gift of self to the service of his bride the church, a gift to be celebrated and valued.

Because the celibate priesthood can only be freely accepted in the light of a deep appreciation for matrimony, good marriages are essential for priestly vocations. As St. Pius' mother shows, her fidelity and the beauty of her vocation helped produce the saintly pope's vocation. Likewise, it was the many families that he served as a parish priest who helped him become the father he was called to be. Priests have the unique opportunity to be members of hundreds of families, and experiencing firsthand the sacrificial love of husbands and wives, of fathers and mothers, teaches the priest how to love his spouse with fervor and devotion.

Often there is a fear in seminarians and priests that the desire for marriage or an attraction for marriage means that one is unfaithful to the vocation God has given them. Or perhaps that they

---

[6] Second Vatican Council, *Sacerdotalis Caelibatus*, 24.

made a mistake. But as any husband or wife will tell you, part of saying yes is saying no to other things, and the goodness of the things you say no to gives depth to the love of the yes. A married woman might be attracted to another man, perhaps a very good and upright man, who might have made a wonderful spouse. But she offers that attraction to the Lord as a gift of love for her husband, and her charity deepens. Likewise, a consecrated man or woman might find marriage attractive at times, but that attraction is one more way that they can offer themselves on the altar of the cross out of love for their spouse the Church. The parallels between the two vocations clearly demonstrate how intertwined they are! Priests learn how to love in the family, and their sacrificial love for the Church then strengthens the families they serve.

An authentic exercise of the priesthood is one of sacrificial love, of laying down one's life for others (cf. John 15:13). This of course is the same as every vocation—every person is called to a life of love, lived out in the midst of the world. The priesthood differs from that of the family in scope, not in kind. The priest is called to lay his life down for the Church. His fatherhood is extended in a particular way and to a wider circle than the fatherhood of a biological parent. But that love in both cases has the same fount, the sacrificial love of God himself, who offered his life in love for each one of us and calls us to lives in relationship with him.

There is a very practical lesson to be learned from this way of loving. Understanding how both married and celibate men and women approach hearts which seem at times to be divided in love is essential to growing in the spiritual life. Our first instinct often when we experience an attraction or a desire which seems to run contrary to our way of life or God's commandments is repression. We think, "I shouldn't feel this way," and we try to drive that feeling deep into our subconscious. Every attraction we feel, however disordered it might be, is rooted in some goodness. And so, instead of strict repression, we can take a different tact; we can offer that feeling to God as a gift of love. If we feel pain at having a divided heart, that makes that gift of love even more precious. By embracing the cross in those moments, and offering our imperfect hearts to God, we allow ourselves to be transformed by his grace and grow in our ability to love fully.

Margherita Sarto was not only speaking about the biological consequences of her marriage when she told her son that he wouldn't have his episcopal ring if she did not have her wedding ring. The love of Christ and of each other which was fostered in that simple Italian family in a very real way produced the vocation of a saintly pope. Their family revealed what the Second Vatican Council would later call the "domestic church," in which "parents should, by their word and example, be the first preachers of the faith to their children; they should encourage them in the vocation which is proper to each of them, fostering with special care vocation to a sacred state."[7]

---

[7] Second Vatican Council, *Lumen Gentium*, 11.

Chapter 11

Pope John Paul I writes a letter to Pinocchio

The Smiling Pope

If there is one thing the average Catholic knows about Pope John Paul I, it is the fact of the brevity of his papacy. Pope for only thirty-three days in the summer of 1978, John Paul I is usually overshadowed by his saintly successor, John Paul II. He briefly captured the world's attention for his smile and genuine personal warmth, and his tragic death from a heart attack in September of 1978 so shortly after his election led many Cardinals to seriously question what God wanted for the Church. Yet one overlooked aspect of Pope John Paul I's history is his extraordinary collection of published letters.

In June of 1972, then Cardinal Albino Luciani wrote a letter to Pinocchio. The future pope, who couldn't count how many times he had reread the puppet's adventures, stopped from his busy schedule to give his childhood favorite some advice.[1] While as a young boy he saw himself in Pinocchio, getting into adventures and scrapes, now a Cardinal in the Church, he saw himself among the list of the puppet's counselors. The future pope wrote, "I will also try to give some to you for your future as a boy, as a young man. Mind you, do not even think of flinging your usual hammer

---

[1] Albino Luciani, *Illustrissimi: Letters from Pope John Paul I* (Boston: Little, Brown and Co., 1978), 72.

at me; I am not prepared to suffer the end of the poor Talking Cricket."[2]

What follows in the Cardinal's letter is a delightful and concise consideration of what it means to grow up, what challenges a boy becoming a man will face, and some simple advice on how to endure that difficult process. The future pope gives the young Pinocchio guidance on what it feels like to have a crush, how to properly seek and embrace autonomy, what to make of doubts about the faith, and the importance of chastity in dating relationships. Along the way, Cardinal Luciani quotes extensively from one of his other favorite books, *David Copperfield*, and holds up the title character as an example for the young Pinocchio. He concludes the letter with a prescient guess at the puppet's vocation, noting that though he had a fairy godmother, when he gets older his fiancée and wife will truly be the source of magic in his life, "unless you become a monk! But I don't see the vocation in you!"[3]

The future Pope John Paul I's letter to Pinocchio is one of many he wrote in a series for the Saint Anthony Messenger published under the title, *Illustrissimi*. The collection features missives to famous figures from Church history like Saint Francis de Sales, St. Therese de Lisieux, and King David, but also to great authors of history like Dickens and Walter Scott, and of course, fictional characters like Pinocchio and Pickwick. At one point he carries on a lengthy series of letters with the great St. Bernard of Clairvaux, writing both sides of the correspondence as the two debate the

---

[2] Ibid., 73.
[3] Ibid., 80.

scope of prudence. "St. Bernard" at one point pokes the future pope, writing, "I see that, in your last remarks, you want to joke. I am in favor of correctness and coherence in public men."[4] The letters are delightfully idiosyncratic and allow the Pope's personality to shine through the pages with a genuineness and simplicity. The collection is a cross between fan mail one might write to a celebrity and sage advice a father might give to a child. In all the vast expanse of papal history, in the libraries of dusty tomes of letters by Cardinals and Popes, these letters are in the running to be the strangest.

An Effective Way to Evangelize

Pope John Paul I's eccentric collection of letters is notable not only for its witty strangeness. He makes the point in a letter to the 19th-century Roman poet Giuseppe Gioacchino Belli that not all evangelization is accomplished through the works of theologians. In the letter, Lucanni describes a conversation he had with a skeptical and pluralistic guest, who seemed to think that all faiths have equal access to the truth and that it's pointless to try and claim one has more truth than another. The remark prompted the Cardinal to dash away from the dinner table for a book of Lev Tolstoy's children's fables and fairy tales. Returning in triumph, he read to the man the famous parable about the blind men who each touch a different part of an elephant and think they know the full truth. The Cardinal then pressed home his point, stating,

---

[4] Ibid., 40.

Listen, it revolts me to think that God sent His Son to say to us: 'I am the way, the truth, and the life,' with the fine result then that all of us find ourselves in the situation of those blind men, each with a wretched little fragment of the truth in his hand, each fragment different from the others. We know the truth of the faith only by analogy, yes; but blind to this degree, no![5]

His guest was stunned into silence at which point Luciani responded, "When Rahner fails, with all his big volumes of theology, Tolstoy can step in with his little fable!"[6]

Pope John Paul I shows in *Illustrisimi* the value of fiction and literature in evangelization. Many of his correspondents were literary figures, either authors or characters, and his genuine love for them and the lessons he drew from them clearly aided his growth in faith. One can talk endlessly through statistics and expert testimonies about the plight of the poor, but more has been done on their behalf through the fiction of Charles Dickens than any thinktank paper. In Dickens, we meet the poor with an intimacy and personality which leaps out of the page and into our hearts. An entire manual of spiritual theology can exhaust all the various ways God leads the soul to heaven, but few can capture so imaginatively and eloquently this transcendent reality as C.S. Lewis's *Voyage of the Dawn Treader*. Philosophers for generations have expounded

---

[5] Ibid., 216.

[6] Ibid. Karl Rahner, SJ was a prolific theologian at the end of the 20th century.

on the importance of the virtues, but many more people learn them subtly from the novels of Jane Austin than from the writings of Marcus Aurelius. And the indescribable scandal of evil is more potent and understandable in *The Brothers Karamazov* than even in Aquinas' treatise *de Malo*.

Literature has a twofold goal which makes it the perfect vehicle for evangelization. On the one hand, its purpose is to satisfy the universal human longing to hear a good story. In that way, it entices us, draws us in, makes us long for more. As Pope John Paul I writes in his letter to the Four Members of the Pickwick Club, "I realized how it was once possible for a dying reader to ask of God, as a special grace, another ten days of life: long enough to receive and read the last installment of the book that immortalized you."[7] Genuine delight attracts and draws the soul. We find ourselves on a journey with incredible companions, and we are willing to walk to the end of the world if need be, so long as the adventure continues.

Literature's second purpose is the exposition of truth. At first glance, of course, the objection is that literature does exactly the opposite. St. Jerome famously reproached himself for reading too much secular literature and threw it all out in favor of scripture. Fiction, the argument goes, leads us into lands of fantasy, castles built on clouds, which might be fun diversions but lack real intellectual seriousness. Better a heavy dose of catechetical memorization to spread the Gospel than madcap stories and foolish daydreams!

---

[7] Ibid., 67.

This way of thinking betrays a superficiality of thought which misses the deep wells of truth we encounter in reading great literature. Fiction must be founded on reality in order to be enjoyable. Characters, even outrageous ones, attract and delight us because they seem real. They express and exhibit some aspect of human nature, and the more authentically they do so the more true and beautiful they seem to us. We feel like we know them—that we would be friends, or enemies, with them in real life, that we would recognize them instantaneously if we walked past them on the street. The fantastical landscape they find themselves in often serves to deepen and explore the aspects of reality that they manifest. Good science fiction, for example, delights not merely because of futuristic technology and exotic planets; rather, the strangeness of the circumstances serves to highlight the truth of human nature which remains constant. Good literature draws us in and then presents us in a new and engaging way with the truth.

The Power of Authenticity

Spending even a little time reading one of John Paul I's letters makes you feel like you know him well. He is nothing if not genuine in *Illustrissimi*. His correspondence reveals stories from his past, his modern television habits, vacation preferences, and even hints at his early romantic side. And in each letter, it is clear that he is holding nothing back. These letters aren't pious facades which show him as a holy and wise bishop; they are authentically Albino Luciani, without reservation or self-consciousness. In that way, they seem to reflect the overarching historical view of the short pontificate of John Paul I: genuine warmth and delight, a pope who was relatable and not clothed in oppressive and imposing pomp. It was John Paul I who was the first to not be crowned with the papal tiara and who in his first angelus address humbly described his terror at being elected pope. A bit of that address is worth quoting here, if only because it shows his genuineness more authentically. The newly elected Pope told the crowd gathered in St. Peters Square,

> Never could I have imagined what was about to happen. As soon as the danger for me had begun, the two colleagues who were beside me whispered words of encouragement. One said: "Courage! If the Lord gives a burden, he also gives the strength to carry it." The other colleague said: "Don't be afraid; there are so many people in the whole world who are praying for the new Pope." When the moment of decision came, I accepted.[8]

We are afraid of being genuine. The prospect of allowing others to catch a glimpse of our souls, of who we really are, fills us with dread. We fear judgment. We fear ridicule. We fear that others won't like us or that others will be turned off by us. We fear being genuine with ourselves, lest we have to accept that portion of ourselves that we wish wasn't there. And when we think about spreading the Gospel, we fear that our faults and our doubts will turn

---

[8] John Paul I, "Angelus Address August 27, 1978," https://vatican.va/content/john-paul-i/en/angelus/documents/hf_jp-i_ang_2708-1978.html

others away from the Good News. So, we become architects who specialize in façades, and we present to the world Potemkin souls which hide reality.

John Paul I's power was in his freedom to be authentically himself. That freedom comes from knowing you are loved by God and in being confident in that relationship. When you know that you are loved not because of your merits but purely because of God's gratuitous goodness, then you are truly free to be open. When your identity is rooted in Christ, then nothing in the world can really shake you. When you know that the love of Jesus will guide and protect you, then there is no need to hide behind a façade. When we allow the words of St. Paul to sink into our hearts, to echo his own conviction, "that neither death, nor life, nor angels, nor rulers, nor things present, nor things to come, nor powers, nor height, nor depth, nor anything else in all creation, will be able to separate us from the love of God in Christ Jesus our Lord" (Rom 8:38-39), then we can truly allow ourselves to be vulnerable and genuine with the world.

Authenticity is a more powerful evangelizing tool than perfection. The person who is free enough to be genuine, even if it reveals faults and failings, is free enough to allow Christ to shine through.

Chapter 12

An Unlikely Reformer

A Scandalous Beginning

It was the height of the Renaissance, and the papacy was mired in scandal. In fact, the reputation of the Pope was so low in the opinion of the people and his actions were so degraded that a modern television adaptation of his life was made out of all the sordid details. The pope was Alexander VI Borgia. According to some contemporaries, he obtained the papacy through political machinations and bribery. He openly flaunted his promise of celibacy and heaped rewards and power on his four children. On May 9, 1490, he celebrated the wedding of one of the most eligible and beautiful young women in Rome, and then promptly started an affair with her.

This chapter isn't about Pope Alexander VI—it's about that young woman, or rather, about her brother. His name was Alessandro Farnese, and his rise to be one of the most important reforming popes is one of the great improbable actions of the Holy Spirit in history. Alessandro's family was typical of Italian renaissance nobility—it was wealthy, well-connected, and ambitious for advancement. Alessandro's own advancement, however, did not look promising. After a classical humanist education, Alessandro found himself in a fight with the powerful Cibo family, a member of which happened to sit on the Chair of Peter: Pope Innocent

VIII. As a result of the quarrel, the young Farnese found himself locked in a tower on trumped up charges that he had plotted to poison members of the Pope's family. Taking advantage of all the commotion surrounding the feast day of Corpus Christi, Alessandro lowered himself by means of a rope from the tower window and fled to safety.[1] But while he was physically safe, his career advancement was stalled so long as Pope Innocent was in power.

Alessandro's situation changed dramatically in 1492 when Rodrigo Borgia, the immensely powerful vice-chancellor of the Holy See, was elected Pope Alexander VI. Gulia Farnese, Alessandro's beautiful sister, had captivated the attention of Cardinal Borgia and had begun an affair with him that continued into his papacy. It was widely known that if you needed something from Pope Alexander, you went to Gulia. A year after his election to the papacy, Pope Alexander named the young Alessandro Farnese a Cardinal Deacon.

Our understanding of what it takes to be a Cardinal and how a Cardinal lives is very much shaped by the modern College of Cardinals. A renaissance Cardinal was a different sort of bird. For one, in most cases Cardinals had not yet received the sacrament of Holy Orders. Modern Cardinals are usually bishops before being given the red hat, with a few exceptions, but for certain all of them are ordained. In many, if not most cases, Renaissance Cardinals enjoyed the title without the sacrament, and delegated clerics to fulfill their sacramental duties for them. Cardinal Farnese was no excep-

---

[1] Gino   Benzoni,   "Paolo   III"   in   *Enciclopedia   dei   Papi*, https://treccani.it/enciclopedia/paolo-iii_%28Enciclopedia-dei-Papi%29/

tion to this convention, and at the most was ordained a deacon at the time he was named a Cardinal.[2]

Likewise, there is an expectation for Cardinals, and indeed all clerics in the Roman Church, to live lives of celibacy, giving their whole selves in service to their bride, the Church. Renaissance Cardinals, and, as we have seen already, Renaissance popes, openly flaunted the Church's rules of celibacy. Again, Cardinal Farnese was no exception. He had at least four children outside of the Sacrament of Matrimony, by multiple women, and he maintained an illicit, and initially adulterous, relationship with an aristocratic Roman woman for some time after being named a Cardinal.[3] Cardinal Farnese was a young, energetic, Renaissance prince. He was not a saintly or pious figure, but one who was ambitious for advancement, money, and who did not deny himself any of the pleasures that were regularly brought before him in his high position. But on May 3, 1512, all that began to change.

The Results of Lateran V

In the long list of ecumenical councils, one of the most neglected is the Fifth Lateran Council, which sat from 1512 to 1517. Part of the reason for its perceived historical irrelevance is the twofold fact that its proposals for reform of the Church were promptly forgotten by the Pope and that almost immediately after its close Martin Luther began the Protestant Reformation. Nevertheless, the

---

[2] Ludwig Pastor, The History of the Popes, vol. XI, (London: Kegan, Paul, Trench, Trubner & Co., 1923), 21.

[3] Ibid., 20.

Fifth Lateran Council was a reform council, called in part to deal with the manifest scandals throughout the Church, and it featured the dynamic interventions of some of the great reforming priests and bishops of the time.

Into this mix of reformers was thrust Cardinal Farnese. He was tasked by Pope Julius II with formally opening the Council and reading the Pope's instructions to the Council Fathers.[4] Along with his intervention, an opening homily was preached by the reforming Augustinian Canon, Giles of Viterbo, who thundered the need for reform and conversion to the assembled notables. Alongside the great Augustinian was another pious reformer, the Dominican Thomas de Vio, also known as Cajetan, whose holiness and scholarship were a driving force in the Council's proceedings. Here were men who believed in the truths of the faith and actually practiced what they preached. One can only imagine the impact of Giles, in his opening homily, warning the assembled bishops and cardinals, many of whom were more princes than priests, that their hearts needed to be converted, and that "[m]en must be changed by religion, and not religion by men."[5]

We can't know for certain what happened in Cardinal Farnese's heart, but the historical evidence shows that he was certainly changed by religion after this point. Sitting there in the council chamber, listening to the decrees that the Council Fathers put forward that Cardinals had to live like the apostles, Cardinal Farnese

---

[4] Benzoni, "Paolo III".

[5] See John W. O'Malley, S.J., "Giles of Viterbo: A Reformer's Thought on Renaissance Rome," in *Renaissance Quarterly*, Vol. 20, No. 1 (Spring, 1967), pp. 1-11.

began to reform his own life.[6] In 1513, he ended his illicit relationship with his mistress and began to practice clerical celibacy. In 1516, he actually moved to the diocese where he was nominally the bishop (he still had only been ordained a deacon at this point) and in 1519 he began a process of reform in his diocese. Also in 1519, he was finally ordained to the priesthood and began true sacramental ministry as a bishop, celebrating his first Mass on Christmas Day.[7] Cardinal Farnese truly had been changed, to the point that the great papal biographer Ludwig Pastor writes, "There is trustworthy evidence that from that time onwards his moral conduct was without reproach."[8]

If the conversion of Cardinal Farnese was the only major result of the Fifth Lateran Council, the Council achieved its end. Though the Church still faced dilettante princes sitting in the chair of Peter for some time afterwards, the most egregious being the Medici Pope Leo X, the seeds of reform had already been planted in the heart of Cardinal Farnese. In 1529, those seeds, which had been germinating for decades, finally bore fruit when at the height of the crisis sparked by Martin Luther, Cardinal Farnese was elected Pope Paul III.

We don't have to delve too deeply into Pope Paul III's papacy to see how much the Holy Spirit was able to do for the Church through this former Renaissance playboy. The new Pope began his papacy by giving extensively to the poor. He approved the establishment of new religious orders dedicated to reform, the most im-

---

[6] Benzoni, "Paolo III".

[7] Ibid.

[8] Pastor, *History*, vol. XI, 21.

portant being the Jesuits. He called some of the greatest minds, and more importantly, real believers in the Gospel, to Rome to help reform the Church. The most famous Cardinal he appointed was the Martyr St. John Fisher, who was beheaded by Henry VIII before he could receive the red hat, but the list of the Pope's appointments included the who's who of church reformers, the most essential being Cardinals Gasparo Contarini, Reginald Pole, and the future Pope Paul IV, Gian Pietro Carafa. The Pope assembled a committee of these bright lights of Church reform, chaired by Contarini, to solve the crises facing the Church. That committee eventually transitioned into the Council of Trent, which Pope Paul III called after tremendous political wrangling in December of 1545. It was at Trent that the first attempts at reform of Lateran V finally came to fruition, and thankfully the Church has never looked back.

God uses the imperfect

Even after his conversion, Pope Paul III wasn't perfect. One of the constant struggles of the Church in the late Renaissance and early Baroque eras was nepotism. Popes would promote their nephews to the rank of Cardinal, and Pope Paul III was no exception. While he worked diligently for the reform of the Church, he also worked for the support of and aggrandizement of his own family. After hearing the epic and moving story of his conversion, our natural tendency is to want to see the pope as a godly hero, acting totally selflessly for the service of the Church. We may be disappointed that he wasn't completely purified and fully perfect after his conversion. After all, hadn't God invited him further? Had he not accepted the grace that God wanted to give him in converting his heart? Were his imperfections the product of further moral failures which grew from a subtle rejection of God's will?

This disappointment in imperfection springs from our disappointment in ourselves. We, too, readily see the spiritual life as a gradual process of self-actualization and perfection, and that at some point we will overcome our imperfections and then be holy. Now we chafe at our weaknesses, but with enough effort and prayer we will one day overcome them. Or, realizing the scope of our faults we turn to despair, thinking that only the saints are the ones who really are perfect, we don't have any hope of achieving that exalted status. Surely, God doesn't want to work in me, to have me be a part of his plan; that's for the holy ones, the monks and nuns and holy desert hermits. Both ways of looking at our imperfections stem from a common misconception of the spiritual life. Our progress in the faith is not a matter of overcoming obstacles but of growing in dependence.

St. John Henry Newman in a homily preached in Dublin noted the curious fact that unlike any other religion, in the Christian faith those who are most admired as saints are the same ones who most fervently profess that they are sinners. He wrote, "Whatever be their advance in the spiritual life, they never rise from their knees, they never cease to beat their breasts, as if sin could possibly be strange to them while they were in the flesh."[9] The saint is never in the position of the Pharisee in the parable, thanking God for his

---

[9] John Henry Newman, "The Religion of the Pharisee, the Religion of Mankind," in *Sermons Preached on Various Occasions* (London: Longmans, Green & Co., 1927), 16.

perfections; he is always like the lowly tax collector, begging God for mercy. This certainty of imperfection on the part of the saints was not a false humility—they really saw themselves as they were, broken and in desperate need of God's grace. Newman continues, "The Catholic saints alone confess sin, because the Catholic saints alone see God."[10] Seen in the light of God's glory, all humanity is broken and inadequate; everyone is imperfect and flawed.

Yet in our flawed state, God chooses to love us and to use us. Or perhaps a better way of putting it is that God chooses to invite such imperfect and frankly ridiculous creatures as ourselves to bring about his kingdom. A helpful analogy is that of the mother teaching her little children to bake a cake. She patiently helps each child scoop the flour and measure the oil and the water, correcting mistakes here and there, cleaning up a multitude of spills, and in general averting culinary disaster. It would be much more efficient for her to make the cake herself, without her tiny helpers. Their little hands can barely keep the measuring cups straight much less fill them to the appropriate level. But despite the difficulties the mother wants her helpers around. She knows that she is really the one baking the cake, and yet, her children can very well say to their father or older siblings later on, "I helped make that cake for you." Objectively speaking, their help was minimal—in fact most of the time it made things worse rather than easier—but still they helped!

God chooses us in our imperfections to be his instruments, not because we are the best tools at hand or the only ones he has to work with, but for our sake, so we can say that we helped. He is not

---

[10] Ibid., 28.

deceived by our own vain imagination of how great we are and how useful we would be to him; he knows the truth about us through and through. He could evangelize, reform, and heal much more effectively on his own, but he is a loving father who wants his children to participate in his great work. Just as he chose Pope Paul III, an imperfect man, to reform his church, he chooses each of us for "some definite service" to bring about his kingdom.[11]

---

[11] Newman, *Meditations and Devotions* (London: Longmans, Green & Co., 1907), 299.

Epilogue

Imploring the Vatican for Baseball Uniforms

The North American College Baseball Team

This final story is only tangentially Papal, but it is delightful, nonetheless. The Pontifical North American College was founded in 1857 to be the seminary for students from the United States in Rome. From the very beginning, the Vatican's intention when founding the seminary was that despite studying in a foreign country, the students maintain their particularly American character.

The seminarians, like many Americans at the end of the 19th century and beginning of the 20th, were obsessed with baseball. The game was still in its infancy when the seminary was founded, but nevertheless it found its way to Rome as early as 1869 when John Schandal, a new seminarian from Newark, showed up at the College with a couple of balls and bats in his luggage.[1] The seminarians loved it from the start, and baseball became the official sport of the seminary. They didn't have much equipment, and couldn't really buy any in Rome, nor did they have a place to play. But most difficult of all, the real cross they were forced to carry for the sake of America's pastime was that as seminarians they were required to wear at all times in public their heavy woolen house cassocks.

---

[1] Robert F. McNamara, S.J., *The American College in Rome: 1855-1955*, (Rochester: The Christopher Press, 1956), 207.

The Seminarians had complained about the uncomfortable cassocks almost since the founding of the seminary. Traditionally in Rome, seminarians of each national college sported a distinct house-cassock, the long usually black garment that priests and altar servers often wear, which identified their nationality and school. When the North American College was founded, they chose a black cassock with blue piping and buttons and a red sash, subtly displaying American colors. The material chosen, however, was heavy and warm, and in the Roman summers incredibly uncomfortable. Forty-two seminarians wrote a petition (another characteristically American way of doing things) to the bishops on the seminary's board of governors asking for a lighter material. They wrote, "It does not seem natural that the same clothing would be equally well-adapted to the dampness and cold of winter, and to the great heat of a Roman summer..."[2] The bishops did not respond, and for years to come the seminarians would have to continue to suffer under the weight of all that heavy fabric.

Even the most uncomfortable and ill-adapted of uniforms did not stop the Americans from playing baseball. The seminarians would pack up their bats, balls, and gloves, and march over to an open meadow in the Villa Borghese, where encumbered by their clerical raiment, they got to playing America's pastime. The sight of a score of young men dressed like priests playing with gusto caused crowds to form, and tourists from the States to marvel at how Vaticanistas knew the American game. Stories would find their way back home about Italian monks playing baseball like pro-

---

[2] McNamara, 176.

fessionals, crisply running the bases and turning double plays.[3] The seminarians in their turn delighted in the ruckus they caused and mischievously caused some more. When the curious onlookers would ask them how they knew the game, the seminarians would prank them by speaking only in Latin.

In 1889, Bishop McQuaid of Rochester came to visit the college, and the seminarians spotted an opportunity to improve their sport sartorial options. Imploring the bishop to intercede on their behalf, the seminarians begged for real baseball uniforms. Bishop McQuaid took their side, asking the rector to make an exception from the strict rule of the house-cassock and to provide the seminary team with more fitting clothes in which to play. After getting the rector's approval, he then sought permission from the Vatican's Congregation for Clergy, who eventually gave their own formal ecclesiastical approval for an exception from the dress code.[4] No longer would they have to play in their heavy loose-fitting cassocks; the Vatican gave approval for the seminary baseball team to wear pants.

Bringing it all together with clothing

I choose this story to conclude because it draws together in itself so many of the varied themes we have seen throughout this short work, and not merely because the young seminarians were

---

[3] Henry A. Brann, *History of the American College*, (New York: Benzinger Brothers, 1910), 231.

[4] McNamara, 303.

given permission to play baseball wearing proper athletic trousers instead of their cassocks. It celebrates the authentic delight and joy that are the hallmarks of true freedom. It emphasizes the role of tradition, both secular and ecclesiastical, and the willingness to suffer (even if it's merely having to wear an uncomfortable cassock) for the sake of the outward signs of the faith. And obliquely it shows the importance of mercy and acceptance of imperfection.

At the risk of self-indulgence, that last point could be expanded on a little more. Baseball is a game particularly suited for the spiritual life, as it is a game of imperfections. The greatest hitters of all time, men like Rogers Hornsby, Ty Cobb, and Ted Williams, only hit four out of ten. The team with the best season record of all time, the 1906 Chicago Cubs, only won 70 percent of their games and lost the World Series. Baseball is a sport that embraces imperfection.

When you look at the vast scope of the men who occupied the Chair of Saint Peter you find the same thing, an institution that embraces imperfection. Christ chose a manifestly imperfect man in St. Peter to be the head of his Church. He was impetuous, bombastic, proud, foolish, and a coward when it counted. The Lord knew all this when he chose him; he wasn't fooled. This was the man who would be the instrument of his grace and the firm rock upon which the faith would be founded. His successors were likewise imperfect. Of the 264 bishops of Rome at the time of this writing, 95 are canonized or in the process of being canonized. The papacy has a saintly batting average of .359, not only not bad by baseball standards, but elite!

Sports writers and skilled athletes will tell you the hardest thing to do in all of professional sports is to hit a major league pitch. It is not for nothing that batting .300 is considered a profound accomplishment! An essential part of the sport is making peace with one's own inadequacies, putting to death one's inherent desire for and expectation of perfection, and taking joy in thirty percent. This mirrors our spiritual lives. Sanctity is even more of a challenge than making hard contact with a baseball. Indeed, it is impossible to attain with our own strength. We cannot bat two hundred on our own strength, much less a thousand. Our weaknesses are too ingrained and our abilities too inadequate. We must rely entirely on grace, and that means putting to death our own perfectionism and, as one spiritual writer has put it, "rejoicing every time [we] discover a new imperfection."[5]

Rather than scandalize us, it should be comforting to us that the "Papal batting average" is so low. Ours is not a church of high achievers; rather, it is a Church of the weak and sinful, those whose strength has failed them and who have no one else to turn to. It is precisely in our imperfections that we see Christ's merciful love the most, and it is only when we see that our strength is truly nothing, that we are finally able to rely on God's grace. Our Church is not founded on the strength of 264 holy men who have flawlessly governed and sustained her. It is founded on the One who entered into our human weakness to meet us there. Our popes, as I hope some of these stories have illustrated, lived incredible lives, but all of

---

[5] J.P. De Caussade, S.J., *Abandonment to Divine Providence*, Ed. J. Ramiere, S.J., (St. Louis: B. Herder Book Company, 1921), 266.

them, especially the saints, were weak and imperfect men, whose own strength was not enough. And yet as Christ reminded his apostle and as the whole Church should be reminded when scandalized or ashamed of our imperfections, "My grace is sufficient for you, for power is made perfect in weakness" (2 Cor. 12:9).

www.ingramcontent.com/pod-product-compliance
Lightning Source LLC
Chambersburg PA
CBHW072013290326
41934CB00007BA/1079